Permanence in
Foster Care

Permanence in Foster Care

A study of care planning and practice in England and Wales

Gillian Schofield and
Emma Ward

with Andrea Warman,
John Simmonds
and Jane Butler

the fostering
network

ADOPTION
& FOSTERING

University of East Anglia

Published by British Association
for Adoption and Fostering
(BAAF)
Saffron House
6–10 Kirby Street
London EC1N 8TS
www.baaf.org.uk

Charity registration 275689 (England and Wales)
and SC039337 (Scotland)

British Library Cataloguing in Publication Data
A catalogue record for this book is available
from the British Library

ISBN 978 1 905664 57 3

Editorial project management by Shaila Shah
Typeset by Avon DataSet Ltd, Bidford on Avon
Printed in Great Britain by The Athenaeum Press

BAAF is the leading UK-wide membership
organisation for all those concerned with
adoption, fostering and child care issues.

Acknowledgements

We would like to thank the Big Lottery Fund, which funded the *Permanence in Foster Care* study on which this book is based, for their support.

We are very grateful to the members of the research study reference group, who gave us the benefit of their expertise, advice and support during the project.

We would also like to thank the many social work practitioners and managers who took the time to complete the detailed questionnaires and to participate in telephone interviews. And we would especially like to thank the foster carers who participated in focus groups and whose words and experiences have enriched this study.

September 2008

LOTTERY FUNDED

Cover illustration

The illustration on the front cover of this book is by Sophie Heyes and is titled *Family*. Sophie lives in a chldren's home and enjoys art, as it helps her to express her emotions. Thanks to Sophie and to Flourish (www.flourish-art.org), a national programme to promote artwork by young people with a history of care, for allowing us to use her illustration.

About the authors

Gillian Schofield is Professor of Child and Family Social Work and Co-Director of the Centre for Research on the Child and Family at the University of East Anglia. She was Chair of the BAAF Research Group Advisory Committee from 2001–2006. An experienced social worker, she practised for some years as a Guardian ad Litem. Her research and teaching interests are in attachment theory and family placement practice, the impact of maltreatment on children's development, the role of long-term foster care as a positive permanence option and the experiences of parents of children in long-term foster care.

Emma Ward is a Research Associate in the Centre for Research on the Child and Family at the University of East Anglia. In addition to her work on the *Permanence in Foster Care* project, she has completed a doctoral study of the motivations of adoptive parents, in partnership with BAAF, and is a researcher on the *Parents of Children in Long-term Foster Care* study, funded by the Economic and Social Research Council and the *Planning for Permanence in Foster Care* study, funded by the Nuffield Foundation, both directed by Gillian Schofield.

By the same authors

Beek, M. and Schofield, G. (2004) *Providing a Secure Base in Long-term Foster Care*, London: BAAF.

Schofield, G. (2003) *Part of the Family*, London: BAAF.

Schofield, G., Beek, M., Sargent, K. with Thoburn, J. (2000) *Growing up in Foster Care*, London: BAAF.

Schofield, G. and Beek, M. (2006) *Attachment Handbook for Foster Care and Adoption*, London: BAAF.

Schofield, G. and Beek, M. (2008) *Achieving Permanence in Foster Care: A Good Practice Guide*, London: BAAF.

Schofield, G. and Simmonds, J. (eds) (2008) *The Child Placement Handbook: Research, policy and practice*, London: BAAF.

Contents

1 **Introduction**

The *Permanence in Foster Care* project (2006–7) was funded by the Big Lottery Research Fund as a partnership between BAAF (the fund holders), the Fostering Network and the Centre for Research on the Child and Family at the University of East Anglia (UEA). The project was managed by Dr. Andrea Warman and Dr. John Simmonds at BAAF, in consultation with Jane Butler at the Fostering Network. Professor Gillian Schofield, Co-Director of the Centre for Research on the Child and Family, led the research at UEA, with Emma Ward as the Research Associate. The project had the approval of the Association of Directors of Children's Services.

A reference group of social work practitioners and managers, with representation from foster carers, met three times during the project, but also helped to design the research instruments as well as commenting on findings and dissemination. A good practice guide (*Achieving Permanence in Foster Care* by Schofield and Beek, 2008) has also been published and complements the contents of this book.

As will become clear from this study, the use of different terminology for "long-term" and "permanent" foster care varies in significant ways across local authorities and within the independent fostering sector. A placement that is described as "permanent" in one authority may be "long-term" in another. This report will use the terms together (long-term/permanent) and separately, but will focus on developing an understanding of the meanings, systems and practices that lie behind the different language.

Policy context

Children who grow up in foster care need the very best care that can be offered. Policy makers, service providers and practitioners need to establish the most effective way to achieve stability as well as good developmental and educational outcomes, for those looked after children who come into care from high risk backgrounds and remain in foster care through to adulthood. As the Government White Paper, *Care Matters: Time for Change* (DfES, 2007a) has emphasised, these long-stay children need the care system to provide them with good quality foster family care, health and education that will help them through childhood to success and fulfilment of their potential in adult life. (Although Wales is not covered by *Care Matters*, it is covered by the same legislation and the Welsh Assembly Government is also concerned to improve the quality of outcomes for children who grow up in foster care in Wales. Welsh local authorities were therefore included in this study.)

Care Matters also suggests that planning for *permanence* will continue to be a priority, stating that 'The overarching purpose of care is to support children to find permanence' (p. 54). Although there are a range of routes to permanence, this means that where a child is expected to remain in their foster placement as part of the family, with no other permanence options (including return home) being considered, the logical position is that this foster placement must be planned and supported as a permanent placement.

Permanence in foster care is perhaps most simply defined as it was in relation to adoption in the Prime Minister's review (Performance and Innovation Unit, 2000, p. 3) i.e.'The security and well-being that comes from being accepted as members of new families'. This definition captures the core elements of *security*, which may be thought of as including both relationship security and stability over time; *well-being*, which includes a range of developmental outcomes; and *family membership* as part of the new family – which will always need to be balanced with continuing membership of the birth family.

Legal context

In contrast to adoption, there is no *legal status* called "long-term" or "permanent" foster care. Because law and guidance do not distinguish between long-term and other kinds of short-term and task-centred foster care, children in long-term foster care (both kinship and unrelated carers) are subject to the same legislation as other children who are looked after in foster care, predominantly the statutes and guidance contained in the Children Act 1989. These have implications for defining foster care planning and placements in terms of permanence.

- Decisions that are made about long-term/permanent fostered children should comply with the welfare check list (s1 Children Act 1989 (CA)), so that both their welfare and their wishes and feelings need to be taken into account.
- Where children in long-term/permanent foster care are looked after under a care order (s31 CA 1989), the local authority has parental responsibility and the right to limit the exercise of parental responsibility by others who may hold it e.g. the birth mother, a birth father who is married to the mother or has gained parental responsibility by agreement or court order, other relatives who have gained parental responsibility, and adoptive parents.
- Where children are looked after but accommodated by voluntary agreement (s20 CA 1989), the local authority does not have parental responsibility in law and those who have parental responsibility (as above) retain it.
- Whatever the legal status of the child, the local authority as corporate parent is bound by the same duty of care under s22, which is 'to safeguard the welfare of all looked after children'.

Whether under a care order or accommodated, children and young people are equally entitled to placement arrangements in foster care that protect them and meet their short and longer term needs. It is important at this stage to bear in mind, therefore, that whatever the legal status of the child in terms of parental responsibility, the child's welfare is paramount. But it is also the case that whatever the legal status of the child, there will be an obligation on the local authority to work constructively with the birth family to promote the child's welfare. It is very important to bear in mind that, as the Children Act 1989 made clear, this is not a question of *parental rights* but of *parental responsibilities*, for both local authorities and birth parents.

Children in long-term/permanent foster care under a care order are diverse in terms of their histories, but evidence will have been accepted by a court that they have experienced or are at risk of significant harm and that a care order is necessary for their safety and wellbeing. For these fostered children, the extent to which local authorities involve birth parents in the detail of the upbringing of their children and in exercising parental responsibility in decision making will have to be a matter for professional judgement in each case, depending on the needs of the child and the capacity of the birth parents to promote the child's welfare.

Long-term/permanent fostered children who are accommodated under s20 come into care for a varied range of reasons, although for all of them there will be a need for the local authority to take steps to keep them safe and promote their welfare. A child with a disability may have become too difficult for parents to care for or a teenager may be out of control and harming himself or others. There will also be children who have experienced significant degrees of abuse and neglect and are looked after under s20, because a parent has been willing to accept the child's need for care. Research suggests that an arrangement for a child to be looked after under s20 may be a caring decision by a parent, a negotiated compromise or a rejection of the child (Schofield, 2000). Under s20 (i), "abandonment" is given as a basis for accommodating a child. In addition, unaccompanied asylum-seeking children are often cared for under s20.

Research context

This project was designed to build on existing research on outcomes for children in long-term foster care and to focus on systems for planning and supporting permanence in foster care. The research on outcomes is limited by the fact that few studies have focused on foster placements that were planned from the start to be long-term foster care in the sense of lasting through childhood to adulthood. Thoburn and colleagues' study of 1,165 placements (Thoburn, 1991) remains the only UK study that was able to use a large sample not only to consider outcomes from placements planned from the outset to be long-term foster care, but also to compare these placements with adoption. This study showed that, once age was taken into account, planned long-term foster placements were just as stable in foster care as in adoption. This positive finding must be viewed in the light of the fact that these were placements through voluntary agencies which were not only planned abut also supported as permanent placements. This would not be true for all foster placements that are currently referred to as long-term.

Schofield and Beek's much smaller longitudinal study of 52 planned long-term foster care placements (Schofield *et al*, 2000; Beek and Schofield, 2004a) found that 75 per cent of the placements lasted at least three years and some of those placements that ended were replaced by further long-term placements that worked well for the children and young people. Both this study and the Thoburn study, a sub-sample of which was also followed up longitudinally (Thoburn *et al*, 2000), showed that, in spite of a lack of biological or legal family ties, carers could be highly committed to parenting their fostered children and that children could became fully part of their foster families. These studies emphasise that the quality of care given to children in these placements needs to be accompanied by a commitment to offering family membership.

Selwyn *et al* (2006) have researched outcomes for children who were in planned long-term foster care, but where this had followed an unsuccessful plan for adoption, including some children who had been adopted but this had broken down. This route will almost certainly have had some implications for the children and the foster families, and in this context just over half (54%) had lasted. Some very important themes emerged from carers in Selwyn *et al*'s study, in particular, the fact that foster carers felt that they had been entrusted with the care and responsibility for these children as part of their family through to adulthood, but had not received the corresponding rights to make a range of simple parenting decisions, such as going on school trips, or to contribute to a range of very important decisions, such as the frequency and nature of birth family contact.

Sinclair *et al*'s large study of foster placements raised some concerns about placement stability, reporting that after a three-year period (1998–2001) 24 per cent of sample children were still in the same placement, with a further four per cent adopted by the same carer (Sinclair *et al*, 2005, p. 129). This study did not report on care plans and did not distinguish between planned long-term foster placements and more short-term, task-centred placements. So some of these moves may have been appropriate and planned. This study, like other studies mentioned here, found evidence of some highly committed and skilled foster carers (Wilson *et al*, 2003). It also found evidence of many children who said that they wanted to stay longer in their placements, particularly up to and beyond the age of 18, raising very important issues about how expectations for post-18 family membership are handled and the role of leaving care teams in promoting continuity in family life.

Sinclair (2005, p. 32) suggested a very helpful model of permanence based on this foster care research, which has four dimensions:

- *Objective permanence* occurred if children had a placement which would last for their childhood and would provide back-up and, if needed, accommodation after the age of 18.
- *Subjective permanence* occurred if the child felt he or she belonged in the family.
- *Enacted permanence* occurred if all concerned behaved as if the child was a family member (e.g. the child was included in family occasions).
- *Uncontested permanence* occurred if the child did not feel a clash of loyalties between foster and birth family.

The principle that permanence has a number of different meanings and has to be looked at on a number of different levels and from the point of view of a number of different parties is an essential part of any policy for achieving permanence in foster care. Each of these permanence dimensions would also require a different kind of assessment, planning and practice when matching children and carers, supporting a placement or identifying when there are problems and finding solutions. But at the heart of the fit between foster care and permanence, Ian Sinclair (2005, p. 123) has argued, we need:

The development of a form of foster care that more nearly approaches a "family for life", which is not seen as "second best" and in which carers can act as parents.

This view of foster care must be understood in the context of a fostering service that is increasingly becoming *professionalised*, not only in terms of the payment of fees, but also in terms of raised expectations of skills, training and post-qualifying education. Professionalism and a family life in which carers act as parents are not incompatible. But there is a need to reconcile and integrate the two identities and sets of expectations.

The other area of research which was relevant for this study was that around care planning and pathways. A landmark study by Lowe and Murch *et al* (2002) which focussed on care planning in adoption and long-term foster care, established the fact that there was a great deal of confusion and uncertainty about what long-term fostering is or could offer to children. They concluded that 'long-term fostering has become something of a Cinderella option' (p. 147), and commented not only on the lack of resources but also the lack of clarity in definitions and systems.

There is a need for policy and planning for long-term fostering to be sharpened up – with clear answers as to what it is and positive reasons for its use. (p. 149)

The problems identified by Lowe and Murch *et al* (2002) have persisted at a national level in terms of lack of clarity about long-term foster care planning and placement. Meanwhile, as Schofield *et al* (2007) found in their UEA study of 24 local authorities, at a local level and in the absence of national guidance, children's services departments, which are required by regulation to have a permanence plan in place by the second looked after children review, have been developing their own definitions, systems and models of planning and practice to achieve stability and permanence in foster care. This *Permanence in Foster Care* study was therefore needed to investigate the nature of these models on a national basis and to learn lessons that would direct future research and inform practice.

2   Aims and methods

This study was designed to build on existing research both on outcomes for children in foster care and care planning more specifically. The primary focus was on investigating systems for planning and supporting permanence in foster care in order to inform future policy and practice and to identify the need for further research.

Aims

- To *map* the range of existing policies and practice models for planning, commissioning, matching and supporting long-term/permanent foster care placements across England and Wales.
- To *investigate* the perceived advantages and disadvantages in practice of different models/services.
- To produce a report that puts these findings in the context of existing research on foster care.
- To develop and disseminate practice guidance, based on new and existing research findings.

Methods

The research project consisted of three phases. The first phase was a national survey that mapped policy, procedures and practice. Question-naires were sent to local authorities and independent fostering providers (IFPs) across England and Wales. Local authorities were then strategically sampled, based on the models of long-term/permanent foster care which had been identified, to ensure that a range of approaches, policies and procedures were represented.

The second phase of the project was further investigation of these models using telephone research interviews with key professionals in these sample local authorities, including fostering and Looked after Children (LAC) managers and social workers, independent reviewing officers (IROs) and panel chairs. This qualitative data supplemented the questionnaire data and allowed for the collection of views of practitioners and managers in the systems.

The third phase of the project, and overlapping with the interview phase, involved conducting three focus groups of long-term/permanent foster carers from local authorities and the independent sector. This allowed for the perceptions and views of service users to be obtained and put in the context of policy and practice.

The second and third phase of the project investigated the perceived advantages and disadvantages of different long-term/permanent foster care planning models and practice.

Questionnaires

The questionnaires were based on issues and research questions identified in the literature. They were piloted with practitioners and further revised following consultation with the reference group. Using contact addresses provided by BAAF and the Fostering Network, questionnaires were sent to 173 local authorities and 145 IFPs in January 2007. The local authorities were sent three separate questionnaires because it was thought that different specialist workers would be more likely to have the expertise to address different areas of planning and practice.

The first local authority questionnaire focussed on planning for children. This asked for information about their definitions of long-term or permanent foster care; the meetings, panels and documentation used in the best interests decision and the match; the nature of support for the placement; parenting roles and responsibilities of foster carers; the role of special guardianship and adoption by carers; and provisions for leaving care. It also included specific questions about how care planning systems dealt with family and friends placements, unaccompanied asylum-seeking children and children accommodated under Children Act 1989 s20.

The second local authority questionnaire focussed on recruitment, assessment, preparation and approval of long-term/permanent foster carers. It included significant specific questions, such as whether newly recruited foster carers would be matched for long-term or permanent foster care as a first placement. The third questionnaire focused on supervision, training and support for long-term and permanent foster carers post-placement. This asked for information about definitions of different types of placement, training, supervision and support, including financial terms and conditions e.g. the basis for varying fees and allowances.

The questionnaire sent to IFPs combined relevant aspects of the three local authority questionnaires, but also asked additional questions about their working relationships with local authorities.

Response rate

There was an overall response rate of 47 per cent (309 questionnaires returned out of 664 sent out). All three questionnaires were returned by 39 per cent (67) local authorities. At least one questionnaire was returned by 54 per cent (93) local authorities. As each questionnaire asked the same core questions about definitions and models, there is good information on the major care planning research questions for all 93 authorities. The response rate for each individual questionnaire is listed below and was just short of 50 per cent for each one.

Local authority: Planning for children 47% (82) (26% paper and 74% electronic)
Local authority: Recruitment and assessment 48% (83) (40% paper and 60% electronic)
Local authority: Supervision and support 45% (77) (40% paper and 60% electronic)
Independent Fostering Provider (IFP) 46% (67) (49% paper and 51% electronic)

Respondents

The majority of respondents for all three local authority questionnaires were managers based in fostering teams, adoption and fostering teams, or permanence teams. Although the child planning questionnaire was expected to be completed by staff in teams responsible for looked after children (and this happened in some authorities), specialist responsibility for permanence in foster care often resided in the fostering service and so they often also completed the child care planning questionnaire. Respondents to the IFP questionnaire were mostly at director or senior manager level.

Size of participant agencies

The number of fostering households in the local authorities ranged from 16 to 685 with the mean number of households being 182. The number of fostering households in independent fostering providers ranged from 10 to 1,950. However, 87 per cent of IFPs which completed a questionnaire (58) had fewer than 100 fostering households. Larger IFPs with offices in different regions have varying degrees of local autonomy, so, as with local authorities, practice is likely to be even more varied than is reflected in the questionnaires available.

Geography and type of local authority and IFP

As Table 2.1 below shows, there was a response from a good geographic spread of local authorities, representing every region from across England and Wales. There was also a reasonable spread of shire, unitary, metropolitan and London boroughs represented.

Independent fostering providers from every region across England and Wales were represented. The biggest group of IFPs were based in the South East of England, but it is important to recognise that some of them have offices in more than one region and the locations represented in this table are typically head offices.

Evaluation of the questionnaire survey response

The final response rate achieved for the questionnaires was more than double the response rate at the initial deadline. It took a considerable number of repeat contacts and reminders from the project researcher to produce the response rate we have. It seemed likely that the fact that respondents could complete a questionnaire electronically or using a hard copy helped to improve the response rate.

Although response rates could, ideally, have been a little higher, this survey is by far the most comprehensive study available of care planning for permanence in foster care in terms of number, type and geographic spread of agencies. The questionnaires were time consuming to complete, but there were few questionnaires with missing data. They have provided a mass of detailed quantitative data for mapping local authorities' policies and procedures and creating a picture of the different models of long-

Table 2.1

Local authorities represented in the questionnaire by type and region and IFPs by region

	LA Shire	LA Unitary	LA Met	LA London boroughs	IFP Region
South East	7	5	0	0	22
South West	4	6	0	0	5
North East	1	3	3	0	2
North West	1	1	9	0	7
Yorks & Humber	1	2	4	0	1
East Midlands	3	4	0	0	3
West Midlands	4	2	5	0	8
East	5	0	0	0	5
Inner London	0	0	0	7	3
Outer London	0	0	0	6	6
Total England	26	32	21	14	62
Wales	0	9	0	0	3
Missing data	0	0	0	0	2

term/permanent foster care. In addition, open questions within the questionnaire asking for clarification and comment provided very helpful and necessary information about the implementation of different systems and the perspectives of service providers.

Telephone interviews

Analysis of the quantitative and qualitative questionnaire data led to the identification of distinctive models of local authority planning, procedure and practice in foster care. A sample of agencies representing these models was identified. Local authority staff from these agencies who completed the questionnaires were emailed and asked if they would take part in a telephone interview. They were also asked to identify other appropriate people for interview from fostering services, looked after children services, independent reporting officers and fostering and adoption panel chairs.

The purpose of the telephone interviews was to follow up and to gain a more in-depth perspective on planning and procedures around long-term/permanent foster care than could be obtained from the questionnaire. Forty-six telephone interviews were conducted with members of staff from 24 different local authorities. The original aim had been 40 interviews in 10 authorities. In practice, we had some authorities with two–three key interviews and others with only one, where we already had questionnaires completed by three different people and only needed additional information from perhaps a panel chair.

Interviewing different members of staff within the same agency allowed for a more detailed and interactive process of investigation. Staff who were interviewed came from all levels within the authority, from senior management to newly qualified social worker. However, the majority were at team manager level. (In this report social work respondents from whatever level are generally referred to as social workers or practitioners.)

Evaluation of the telephone interviews

Since complexity of ideas, attitudes and terminology proved to be at the heart of different definitions and procedures, the process of interview discussion provided very useful data. Most interviews were very lively and informative. They confirmed some aspects of the questionnaire data, offered clarification of other points and pointed us to issues, such as the significance of age in planning, the leaving care services and the perceived potential role of special guardianship orders that questionnaires had not stressed to the same degree. As this report shows by the use of quotation, interviews provided some of the more vivid sense of managers' and practitioners' activities and concerns.

Foster carer focus groups

Focus groups were undertaken during the project in order to understand the planning, approval, support and meaning of long-term/permanent placements from the foster carers' perspective. Although there have been previous studies of foster carers' views on permanence using focus groups (Beek and Schofield, 2002), it was important to get up-to-date views of this rapidly developing field, to have groups of carers, all of whom had experience of providing these types of placements, and to consult groups in areas that would reflect regional differences and a range of ethnicities and cultural backgrounds. The topics explored in the focus groups were identified from previous literature, but also from issues arising from the questionnaire data.

Three focus groups were undertaken with foster carers from local authorities and the independent sector who had cared for at least one child placed with them in a long-term or permanent placement. The focus groups ranged in size from 10 to 22 foster carers, were ethnically diverse, and included male and female, new and experienced carers. The focus groups were held in London, Birmingham and Cardiff, with each being jointly run by representatives from BAAF or the Fostering Network and from the UEA research team.

Evaluation of the foster carer focus groups
The focus groups were very successful in raising issues that were of immediate importance for foster carers and for foster children and young people. The timing of the focus groups, after the survey had been analysed and alongside the interview phase, made it possible to include key issues that had arisen from the questionnaire data for discussion (such as contact, parental decision making and leaving care), then feed ideas from the focus groups back into telephone interviews. As with the interviews, the use of quotations in this report from over 40 foster carers in just three focus groups has provided vivid insights into foster carers' experiences.

Analysis and reporting

The questionnaire data were analysed using the SPSS software package and the data from the telephone interviews and focus groups were analysed using the NVivo software package. Detailed qualitative comments were also provided in the questionnaire data and have contributed to the analysis and research report. The questionnaire, interview and focus group data are reported together by topic throughout the report.

Statistics are used selectively throughout the report, with as much explanation as is possible of the significance of findings. Percentages are rounded and so will not always add up to 100. Sample sizes vary depending on the groups and sub-groups that are being referred to and care has been taken to ensure that, where claims need to be modest because of a lack of statistical significance, this is stated. The statistics given do not always refer to the full 93 local authorities which took part, as some questions only appeared in one of the questionnaires, and not all questionnaires were returned from all authorities; also for some questions there were missing data. However, this project was designed as broadly speaking a descriptive study rather than an outcomes study and we were looking for as good an understanding as could be achieved of the many different practices that are being developed across the country.

The report of the findings begins with an exploration of the definitions and models of care planning for permanence in foster care that emerged. This includes: the terminology used to define and explain long-term/ permanent placements; expected length of placement; any policies on age and choice of placement; children accommodated under s20; unaccompanied asylum-seeking children, and family and friends carers. Care planning for long-term/permanent placements is discussed and includes findings on the different use of fostering and adoption panels and meetings and documentation in planning for long-term/permanent foster care. Post-placement support and work with children through to leaving care are also covered, including team structures, visits, parenting roles and leaving care provision.

Findings on the fostering service include recruitment methods, preparation and approval of long-term/permanent foster carers. The supervision, training and support, including financial provision, for long-term/permanent foster carers is also discussed. Finally, views on legal permanence options which foster carers could take up for children in long-term/permanent placements, in particular special guardianship, are considered in the light of data from all aspects of the study.

All respondents and agencies have been anonymised. Where quotations from interviews are used, social work respondents in local authorities are designated as Fostering (fostering teams) or LAC (teams with case responsibility for looked after children). The additional designation of "single" and "dual" will become clear from the analysis of models in Chapter 3. Where quotations are from questionnaire data, this is indicated – this is most common for IFPs which were not included in the interview phase as they are not generally responsible for child care planning systems, but which offered detailed comments on the question-naires. Foster carer quotations are all from the focus group transcripts.

3 Definitions and models of permanence in foster care

Terminology and systems

The most striking finding to emerge from the study was the development across England and Wales of two quite different models or systems for providing permanence in foster care (see Table 3.1). The majority (61%) of local authorities have a *single system* of foster care described as *either* long-term foster care (53%) or permanent foster care (8%). But a significant minority (39%) have a *dual system* of both long-term *and* permanent foster care, with different definitions and often different policies and planning procedures for each. It is also of note that there was good representation from Welsh authorities from both dual and single system authorities.

Table 3.1

Local authorities with single or dual systems

	Single	Long-term single	Permanent single	Dual	Total
LA	57 (61%)	49 (53%)	8 (8%)	36 (39%)	93 (100%)

The analysis in this report focuses on the distinction between single and dual systems, with long-term single and permanent single being collapsed together. This decision was taken in part because of the low numbers (8) of local authorities with a single system for permanent foster care. But it was also because where local authorities had a single system, this was described as their foster care permanence option, whether it was called long-term or permanent foster care. It was also the case that in the questionnaires and in the interviews for single system authorities, respondents were often making it clear that the terms were used interchangeably. For example:

> *I think we try and use the term permanency, but I have used it inter-changeably [with long-term foster care] in this conversation and I think lots of people would use it interchangeably.* (LAC, single)

A number of *variables* were looked at to see if they were associated with the single and dual system planning models. For example, there was no significant association between the size of authority, judged by the number of fostering households, and whether the local authority had a single or dual system. There was also no significant association between systems and the type or size of local authority (metropolitan, unitary, shire, London borough).

Independent fostering providers (IFPs) are providers of placements and so do not have separate child care planning systems as such. However, the survey showed that they do, nevertheless, vary in their use of single and dual terminology and models.

Table 3.1
Independent fostering providers with single or dual systems

	Single	Long-term single	Permanent single	Dual	Total
IFP	21 (31%)	18 (27%)	3 (4%)	46 (69%)	67

A greater proportion of IFPs than local authorities have both long-term and permanent placements. This almost certainly reflects the fact that most IFPs will have arrangements with more than one local authority and will therefore have to fit into more than one system. However, certain IFPs did take quite a specific line on permanence and had single or dual systems defined explicitly within their own policies. Some providers were also approved adoption agencies or specialised in providing permanent foster placements and were particularly likely to have a clearly articulated view on applying concepts of permanence to foster care planning.

An important finding was the impact on the relationship between the independent sector and local authorities of the *diversity* of systems in local authorities. IFPs needed to provide placements that could variously be defined as long-term and permanent by different local authorities, but with very different meanings and expectations. This could have an impact at the contractual level of commissioning, tendering and partnership arrangements with different local authorities, but could also have implications at the level of the individual foster home. An IFP carer could be caring for three children from different authorities with different terminologies and expectations, not only of procedures but also of the very nature of the relationship between the foster family and the child.

In both local authorities and the independent sector, it was clear that although some signs of terms being interchangeable existed, strong views were held by some individuals in relation to both terminology and systems. Characteristic views in favour of a single/long-term foster care system might be expressed in positive terms such as 'Long-term foster care is a positive permanent option and should not be seen as second choice' through to more negative reasoning, such as, 'A foster placement can never be truly permanent without a legal order so we have to call it long-term'. In contrast, one respondent from a single/permanent authority defended the use of the term "permanent", saying on the questionnaire, 'You cannot call it "long-term" foster care because that sounds like it has an end. The last time I used the expression "long-term" was when I parked my car at the airport.'

Those with dual systems were often equally emphatic about the necessity of having two routes, in order to reflect the distinction between "permanent" foster placements that were closer to adoption in terms of expectations of family membership into adulthood and "long-term" placements that were more equivocal in terms of whether the young person might be expected or enabled to make a long-term commitment to being a member of the foster family into adult life.

Such factors in these definitions and models will now be looked at in more detail as they are very much at the heart of the search for clarity in relation to what is expected of a foster placement that is part of a permanence plan.

Defining the expected length of the foster placement

Because the concept of permanence has within it the notion of a family that will last for some time or even become a "forever" family, *the length of placement* envisaged in different definitions of long-term and permanent foster care is central. This can be understood in relation to the child's *age* (e.g. up to or beyond 18), *legal status* (e.g. up to leaving care) or *life stage* (e.g. "independence", adulthood).

Terminology and definitions of length of placement did not go together in an entirely predictable way, but the choice of definitions tends to be influenced by the model. Table 3.2 shows how local authorities with different systems defined the expectations of the length of a long-term and permanent placement. Practitioners could tick as many of the definitions of length which applied to their system as they wished.

Table 3.2
Local authority definition of length of placement in single and dual systems

Local authority definition of length of placement	*Single (n = 54)*	*Long-term dual (n = 25)*	*Permanent dual (n = 25)*
Caring for the child where there is no plan to move the child	61%	56%	60%
Caring for the child up to a certain age (age not specified in 34 cases and specified as 18 in 12 cases)	54%	48%	20%*
Caring for the child until they leave care	83%	88%	48%**
Caring for the child as part of a family into adulthood	80%	36%	92%**

* Significant at the $p < 0.05$ level
** Significant at the $p < 0.01$ level

There was no significant association between systems and including a definition of long-term or permanent care as 'caring for the child where there was no plan to move the child'. Just over half of all authorities included this as *part* of their definition of long-term and permanent care. For the single systems and for long-term foster care in the dual system, significantly more local authorities stated that long-term/permanent foster care was 'caring for the child up to a certain age', typically 18[1] and 'caring for them until they leave care',[2] compared to permanent foster care in the dual system.

In local authorities with dual systems, permanent foster care was more likely to be defined as 'caring for the child as part of the family into adulthood' compared to their long-term placements. However, local authorities with single systems for long-term or permanent foster care were also likely to define a placement this way.[3] This is logical in that dual system authorities want to emphasise the permanent nature of the permanent foster care route and to distinguish it from long-term foster care, while single route authorities want to emphasise that this is foster care as a permanence option.

It does appear that for *a minority* of local authorities with single systems, the expected length of a long-term/permanent placement may vary from, at one end of the spectrum, having a plan not to move the child to the child being considered part of the family into adulthood, depending on the individual circumstances. Indeed, over three-quarters of local authorities with the single system ticked more than one definition of length for long-term/permanent foster care (78% 42). This could indicate overlapping definitions or definitions that were flexible, including rather different children with a long-term care plan. Confirmation of possible degrees of flexibility arose in the interview data.

I would define it [long-term foster care] as being up until whatever was appropriate for that young person. It might be that they remain there, that they go on to college or university and they go into some sort of supported lodgings with a foster carer or it could be that they

---

[1] $\chi2 = 8.06$, $df = 2$, $p<0.05$
[2] $\chi2 = 14.29$, $df = 2$, $p<0.05$
[3] $\chi2 = 22.65$, $df = 2$, $p<0.01$

leave at an earlier age, go into some sort of independent living. So it is according to the needs of the child. (Fostering, single)

The findings from the questionnaire suggest that authorities with a dual system expected that if a child was placed in a *permanent* placement, that placement would last into adulthood, whereas in a *long-term* placement, definitions were more likely to be until they left care or where there was no plan to move them. This need to make a clear distinction where there were two options was demonstrated in the interview data.

What we are kind of encouraging for permanent placements is that the day the match is taken to panel is celebrated in a similar way to an adoption and that it is a real marker of "you are here forever" . . . I think long-term foster care is the default position for those children where they are in a placement and it is certainly the placement that they are very likely to remain in but . . . where actually the likelihood is that they are going to go home when they are 16 or 17, that is going to be their choice and they have been safeguarded for maybe a number of years in the local authority looked after system through that. (IRO, dual)

In every sense here, the long-term placement is viewed in this dual system as less of a commitment than a permanent placement – being described as a 'default position', where children are 'very likely to remain' but where there is no sense of this as a definite care plan. Children have perhaps been 'safeguarded' rather than becoming part of the family. As will be discussed later, this approach raises some key questions as to whether an eventual return home would be based on an assessment of the young person's best interests or based simply on an expectation or acceptance that this is what the young person will choose to do. Some practitioners argued that this was just the reality and needed to be acknowledged. (Age and links to permanence planning are discussed further below.)

Independent fostering providers showed similar patterns to the local authorities in the way in which they defined long-term and permanent care in relation to the length of placement. IFPs with single systems stated that the length of placements could vary, whereas IFPs with dual systems were more likely to be specific in order to demonstrate the differences i.e.

permanent foster care was more likely to be seen as caring for the child into adulthood[4] and long-term foster care more likely to be until independence,[5] a certain age[6] or with no plan to move.[7]

Table 3.2.
Differences in IFP definitions of the length of placements

	Single (n = 19)	Long-term dual (n = 45)	Permanent dual (n = 44)
Caring for the child where there is no plan to move the child	90%	80%	59%*
Caring for the child up to a certain age (age not specified in 42 cases and specified as 16 in 1 case and 18 in 14 cases)	63%	60.%	34%*
Caring for the child until they leave care	90%	76%	52%**
Caring for the child as part of a family into adulthood	95%	47%	93%**

* Significant at the p<0.05 level
** Significant at the p<0.01 level

A significantly greater number of IFPs defined long-term foster care in the single and the dual system as placements where there was no plan to move the child compared to local authorities,[8] with over 80 per cent of IFPs doing so compared to around 60 per cent of authorities. IFPs have a contractual arrangement with the local authority and although they indicated on their questionnaires their active role in assessing children in their placements and contributing to planning, the local authority is in control of the length of the placement and has the power to change the plan.

---

[4] $\chi2 = 30.19$, $df = 2$, $p<0.01$
[5] $\chi2 = 10.29$, $df = 2$, $p<0.01$
[6] $\chi2 = 7.57$, $df = 2$, $p<0.05$
[7] $\chi2 = 8.08$, $df = 2$, $p<0.05$
[8] $\chi2 = 9.14$, $df = 1$, $p<0.01$

Some long-term placements are, in effect, permanent but cannot be planned as such, as local authorities will not commit. (IFP, question-naire)

Some IFP managers commented in the questionnaire that this degree of uncertainty could cause children anxiety, a point also presented in the focus group, as this IFP foster carer describes.

You think they are there until 16 ... 18 ... but it is always in the background as well, what if the funds aren't going to be there, because you are employed by a private agency? You then think, well, what if this child is here for so many years and suddenly they say well, we can't afford, you know, to keep you there ... What happens then? And that worried me a lot that he thinks he is here for good and you tell him as much as you can, you know, you say yes, you are here now until you leave and go off, but they are having a shake around in the social services where he is from and he doesn't know what is going on and you do worry that are they suddenly going to pull the plug on it ... it is a worry, all that. (Foster carer)

The significance of age for the choice of foster care plan

Just under a third of local authorities (31%, 24) stated that they had age limits regarding plans for long-term or permanent foster care. There were no significant differences between long-term/permanent single/dual systems in terms of numbers using age limits. Only four IFPs had age limits for long-term/permanent care, which is not surprising perhaps considering that IFPs provide placements for a range of local authorities; 'Local authorities have different policies and we go along with them' (IFP questionnaire).

There was no clear pattern or consistency in the actual age limits across local authorities. However, the interview data showed that age was, in practice, a very influential factor in planning long-term and permanent foster care placements, regardless of whether there were explicit or implicit age limits formally built into the model. This is consistent with other research (Lowe and Murch *et al*, 2002). All the practitioners interviewed not only had expectations about how the age of children might affect the adoption or long-term foster care choice, but also about the differing needs and expectations of long-term or permanent foster placements for children placed at different ages.

Age and related factors in the adoption or long-term foster care choice

All practitioners interviewed stated that, for most children younger than around six or seven, the plan of first choice would be adoption rather than long-term or permanent foster care. All stated that the vast majority of children over ten would be placed in foster care rather than adoptive families. Regardless of their different foster care planning systems, practitioners agreed that, if it was likely that the child could not be returned home, the best option for most young children would be legal permanence in the form of adoption, if it could be achieved, rather than remaining in care. But they also recognised that, for children aged above seven (and with some agencies children aged five or six), it was harder to find adoptive homes.

> *Adoption will always be sought in preference to long-term fostering, but sometimes you have to say maybe we're not going to find anybody because the child's too old or maybe the behaviour's too difficult.* (IRO, dual)

> *At eight years old, it becomes much more difficult for the agency to find adoptive families and it seems more possible to identify a long-term foster family for those children. Invariably, another factor that comes into play with those children is that they might have experienced longer periods of neglect and abuse and moves from their earlier years with their birth families. So they often need foster carers that can offer them not just a family life, but also therapeutic parenting. Such children often need ongoing support from the local authority as well as other services and their carers also would need the support from their agency. As a result of all that, the plan then is for permanency for those children via long-term fostering. Sometimes if there is a child of a particular ethnicity, this might on some occasions mean that it is more difficult to find adopters from a*

particular ethnic group and so that might be another influencing factor. (Panel chair, single)

Age is thus linked to other factors – such as length of abuse history, disturbed behaviour and the resultant need for therapeutic foster care and support for children and their carers. Achieving the right match in relation to ethnicity and culture for children of a certain age also affected the choice of adoption or foster care. These findings confirmed that the picture presented in the Lowe and Murch *et al* (2002) study persists. So also does the influence of practitioner views that children in middle childhood and above would be likely to have higher levels of contact and "stronger" relationships with their birth family, leading to a long-term foster care choice.

> *I think it's because of their relationship with their birth family and the feeling that children wouldn't be able to accept adoption because of their loyalty to their family and their attachment. I think that is something that could change in time, you know, when children settle, but certainly the Guardian at the moment is feeling very strongly that it should be long-term fostering rather than adoption.* (LAC, single)

Here there are a number of different discourses – in particular, the two concepts of "loyalty" and "attachment" to the birth family that often get merged in this way but need to be separated out. Views of these factors varied greatly between social workers and it seemed likely that courts would be getting very different perspectives on key issues. Whatever the system or set of beliefs about adoption or foster care as permanence options, developmental assessments of need in each individual case remain a matter of professional knowledge and judgement. The quality of that judgement depends on a good understanding of child development, in the context of foster care research. But as Sinclair (2005, p. 22) has suggested, 'Research assists judgement. It is not a substitute for it'.

Some practitioners reported that younger children may be placed for permanence in foster care placements because they had exceptional special needs or were part of a sibling group which it was felt was best to keep together (factors also mentioned in Lowe and Murch *et al*, 2002).

Obviously for the very young children we probably wouldn't be looking at permanent foster care, we would be looking at adoption. Although for some young children we do go for permanent foster care, for example, if they are part of a sibling group where there is quite a wide age range it might be difficult for us to find adoptive carers for them all together. (Panel chair, single)

Special needs additional to age were highlighted by some foster carers as reasons why long-term or permanent foster care might be planned. However, they also noted that their local authority still wanted to promote "legal permanence" once the child was settled.

The two boys with Foetal Alcohol Syndrome I care for – we were really being pushed to adopt them to give them this [legal] permanency and our attitude wasn't the fact that we didn't want to adopt them, but we didn't want to take them out of the system because of the support. (Foster carer)

Some practitioners expressed the view that, for some children, long-term or permanent foster care should be seen as the best option and should be valued equally with other types of legal permanence.

It is maybe not a case of it being second best – it is more a case of how it matches the child's needs and for some children adoption just wouldn't be useful or helpful. (LAC, single)

In the focus groups, foster carers, who also had adopted or birth children, commented that they felt that children who were in foster care did not perceive the placement as functioning differently or being experienced as second best – and nor did they as carers and parents.

When [foster son] went long-term we were delighted. You know, he is a smashing lad. I personally didn't feel any different towards him. We bring him up as our son, just as I did with my [adopted] daughter so it didn't feel any different mentally for me. (Foster carer)

Although *Every Child Matters* (DfES, 2003, p. 45) stated that there was a 'need to ensure that different permanence options are equally credible including long-term fostering', there still appears to be a strong culture of perceiving legal permanence as the goal for all children. This leaves some areas of concern about the impact of that culture on children beyond early childhood who are far more likely to be placed in foster care. Children in long-term/permanent foster care and their carers may feel that their route is regarded as second best or even as a last resort. The fact that return home and adoption are considered first should not necessarily mean that foster care is a devalued option. But procedural and practice messages that then follow for those in foster care need to make the option *feel* legitimate. This is not easy if carers feel under pressure to adopt or apply for special guardianship (discussed below) and messages are given, explicitly or implicitly, that this is because being in foster care, having social workers and being reviewed is not only impermanent but generally undesirable for children.

Age and expectations for children in long-term/permanent placements

In defining the different placement options, children placed in long-term or permanent foster care were typically thought of by both social workers and managers as falling into two distinct age groups – middle childhood and adolescence. These two groups were thought to have quite different needs from permanency planning and their placements were seen therefore as serving different functions and having different expectations. What was also clear was that for both age groups, beliefs and expectations were quite closely linked to the debate about the meanings of "long-term" and "permanent" foster care in single and dual model authorities.

Children in *middle childhood*, between the ages of six or seven and about eleven or twelve, with a plan to remain in foster care, were generally seen as having special needs for care (mainly as a result of emotional and behavioural problems), but also as likely to be having regular and probably frequent contact with their birth family. However, in this age group, *both* long-term *and* permanent carers in most authorities were expected to offer a high level of foster family membership and commitment and the placement was expected to last into adulthood. There was also an acknowledgement that it was not enough to have systems that reflected these definitions and expectations – messages for children had to be practical and explicit.

> *I encourage foster carers to say to children even if they're only ten . . . 'When you're 18 we'll have a big party' and when they're very committed, 'I expect you'll be bringing your children to see me one day', and all that kind of thing. Because just to say "permanence" to them is meaningless. But they can think about 18 and learning to drive . . . and I say to them or ask the foster carers to say to them, 'We'll have to save up for driving lessons for you', and all that kind of thing so that they can think way ahead.* (IRO, dual)

Some social workers and foster carers (from both local authorities and the independent sector) of children who had been placed in middle childhood considered the children to be full members of the foster family and found that children felt the same way too, sometimes referring to the carers as 'mum and dad' and often talking about them as parents. This did not exclude acknowledgement of the importance of the birth family – but it did often mean playing down the formal status of the family as a foster care placement.

> *He has got a book and pictures of his birth mum and everything in it. But he wants to call Lisa [carer] mum. He calls me dad some days, some days he calls me Bill, whatever mood he is in. But it has given him a sense of permanency – it is his family. His brothers and sisters are our own children; they are not his "foster" brothers and sisters. We don't even mention the word "foster care" in the house – it doesn't exist.* (Foster carer)

Social workers generally hoped that, for children placed in middle childhood, a long-term or permanent placement would bring not only stability and well-being, but also acceptance as a member of the new family, very much as anticipated in the definition of permanence in adoption in the Prime Minister's review (Performance and Innovation Unit, 2000), quoted above. The objective of most placements in middle childhood for many practitioners was to achieve "subjective permanence" (Sinclair *et al*, 2004; Sinclair, 2005), that is, the children conceived of the family as their own and felt as if they belonged to it. From some of the foster carer data it would appear that these foster carers also defined the placements and their role in terms of demonstrating "enacted permanence", that is, where all concerned behaved as if the family were a lasting unit, including the child in family occasions and the child considering the foster family to provide them with a mum and dad, brothers and sisters in addition to their biological, emotional and legal ties to their birth family.

Although the overwhelming message from questionnaires, telephone interviews and foster carer focus groups was that children in middle childhood needed permanence in terms of family membership and mutual commitment between child and foster family through to adulthood, there were some views expressed that even quite young children – aged six or seven and certainly by nine or ten – had such "strong" ties to their birth families that they would not invest in this new family. Sometimes, this view was expressed in terms of the child having a "primary attachment" to the birth family, often linked to a concept of "loyalty" to the birth parent – a combination discussed earlier.

If they are ten or something plus, then they probably, you know, they have got very established attachments and links to their birth families. So by the time they get any older, you know it is very hard to shift that really. (Fostering, single)

This view was influential not only in choosing foster care over adoption, but might lead to a very significant difference in approach to planning foster care that would be likely to affect a whole range of messages to the child, to the foster family and to the birth family. It would also be likely to lead to different approaches to contact or decision making that would, for some children, mean perhaps prioritising the birth family and leaving foster carers in rather an uncertain role. In dual system authorities, such an assessment of 'hard to shift' attachment and links, as this social worker put it, might lead to a child being placed for long-term rather than permanent foster care.

The basis for this assessment, that some middle childhood children cannot be expected to form significant attachment relationships in a foster family, would seem to be a belief that some children are so "strongly" attached to their birth parents that even at the age of six or seven they would not be prepared to or able to form a new selective attachment to the foster carers with whom they were to be placed till adulthood. This would appear to be a misreading of current attachment theory and research, which offers a more subtle picture of evolving and multiple attachments in middle childhood (Kearns and Richardson, 2005). Developmental theory and research would indeed suggest that children can be expected to be "strongly" attached to birth parents; they are biologically pro-grammed to look for closeness and comfort even from maltreating care-givers. However, in circumstances of abuse, neglect and insensitive parenting, this "strong attachment" is likely to be an insecure attachment (Howe, 2005; Schofield and Beek, 2006). But even if the relationship with the birth parents were to be meeting some of the child's emotional needs, this would not be a barrier to the child *also* forming an attachment rela-tionship, hopefully of a more secure kind, with the new carers (Schofield and Beek, 2008). The challenges for these children can be overcome by sensitive and effective carers and with good social work support – as documented in Wilson *et al* (2003) and Beek and Schofield (2004a).

It is therefore important to distinguish here between a foster care permanence plan that *takes into account* the benefits and difficulties presented by a child's relationship with the birth parent, and a plan that appears to place a primary *value* on that relationship or *accepts*, rather fatalistically, that a young child will never be able to move on emotionally to healthier, more secure relationships. Practice models reported in this study seemed at times to make explicit or, more often, implicit judgements about the psychology and developmental needs of children. These need care and investigation, as they may become taken for granted in ways that do not reflect the research or the range of individual children's experiences and needs in this age group.

The questionnaire and interview data on *adolescents* were also very detailed in relation to the interaction between *definitions and models* used by local authorities and IFPs and the *perceived needs and expectations* of *adolescents* in foster care. What was, however, often taken for granted in responses was that the population in question were adolescents newly admitted to care in the teenage years. These adolescent entrants (Sinclair *et al*, 2007) are a significant group of young people to assess and manage in foster care and present real challenges in relation to conceptualising and implementing a permanence policy. They will also be diverse in terms of whether they are coming into care as a result of abuse and neglect or as a result of their own difficult behaviours or, as is common, a combination of these factors. In what sense might the new foster care plan for these young people be defined as "permanent"?

However, there is another group of adolescents in need of a new plan and placement who may have already been separated from their birth families for a number of years. These include young people who may have come into care in the pre-school years or in middle childhood. Some of these young people will have had an experience of a succession of short-term placements or of a planned or unplanned long-term placement that has ended or both. There will also be teenagers who come into care from adoptive families that have run into difficulties in the adolescent years. These different groups will all have varied profiles and needs (Beek and Schofield, 2004a; Sinclair *et al*, 2005) which challenge the different models and systems that decide on a care plan – in what sense might the new foster care plan for these young people too be defined as "permanent"?

Young people who enter the care system as adolescents were likely to be between the ages of 12 and 15, with children of 16 and above rarely entering care. They were also seen as likely to have significant, sometimes referred to as "strong", relationships with their birth families, which were expected to dominate both initial plans and likely outcomes. Placements were therefore expected in the main to last until the child left the care system, either to return to the birth family or to move into independent living. Practitioners stated that because young people still identified very much with the birth family, they would inevitably seek to live with them or live independently when they are able. Some of the foster carers identified that this was true for some of the children in their long-term/permanent care.

> *I have got a 13-year-old at the moment you know, he is the youngest one in placement but I think he knows he is living with me for as long as he allows it because he says to me 'when I am 16 I am going to be living with my father'. (Foster carer)*

But research has found that, although this may be the talk in the early years of an adolescent placement and the young person may indeed return home, it is not unusual for the birth family not to be prepared to accept the young person back when the age of 16 or 17 is reached or to accept them home only for it to break down (Farmer *et al*, 2004; Sinclair *et al*, 2005). The expectation of an inevitable return home, that had become built (again often implicitly rather than explicitly) into definitions and planning systems, tended to be seen as driven by what the young person would want and do rather than an assessment of what would actually be in their best interests in the longer term. But although what young people want is a major factor in placement success (Sinclair *et al*, 2007), the practitioner expectation of inevitable return home raised important questions about what were thought of as "temporary" placements alongside young people's need for a permanence plan in the form of a supportive family.

> *These are children who don't want a new family; they just want somewhere to live until they can leave care. They are not looking for that ongoing relationship with a foster family. So they are more likely to be children who come into care at a later age, you know, twelve plus, and who may have bounced around the system a few times before landing somewhere that they are happy. So they are likely to be, you know, disaffected teenagers. What this means is that once we say, look, we are going to keep those young persons long term, the fostering team are no longer looking for a different placement. They are not saying this is a temporary placement, we have got to find somewhere else, we are saying OK this is a temporary placement, it seems to be working, we will leave them there.* (Fostering, dual)

This approach valued the notion of finding a placement that worked well, where the young person could be happy and from which they would not be moved. But the premise was that the young person did not want "a new family". It was not always clear from the contexts to this and similar accounts whether this was because the birth family was active and useful to the young person or whether it was more a matter of the young person's sense of "loyalty". It was also not clear whether it was the young person or the practitioners and managers who believed that it was not possible to have relationships with or feel part of more than one family. This is a key question since feeling "part of the family" is central to the way in which permanence is usually defined. In this context there could often be some confusion between managing multiple family loyalties and managing multiple attachment relationships – and it seemed at times as if for this age group too a view of attachment as being limited to one family might be getting in the way of more flexible thinking (Schofield and Beek, 2008).

What was clear, though, was the likelihood that in all planning systems and models, adolescent placements would start as a temporary placement and then work out or not work out rather than being an intended and planned long-term match at the point of placement. One factor here was that it was the exception rather than the rule to have a range of teenage placements to choose from in order to make a match. But more significantly the assumption that teenagers did not "need a new family" was influencing expectations about the importance of permanence in terms of family membership. Inevitably, with a number of adolescents being described as having characteristics such as not being suitable for placement with younger children because of sexually aggressive or anti-social behaviour, matching might often have to be on grounds of mutual protection rather than longer-term emotional needs. However, a number of these young people may need a foster family to offer support to them into adult life, if at all possible, and they might present a greater risk to themselves and others without it.

Also in this age range (12–15) will be some young people coming into care for the first time who are long-term victims of neglect and physical, emotional and sexual abuse in their birth families. They may never have experienced family life that is supportive and protective, with mutual respect and prosocial values. Whether or not these young people are primarily thought of as a threat to others or as vulnerable to others or both, there must be some concerns about planning models that accept the young person's own prioritising of the birth family without attempting to offer alternative committed family experiences that might equip the young person better for adult life. Some local authorities and independent providers, but it appeared to be a minority, were aware of this issue and in the light of such concerns were very clearly trying to focus on securing a sense of permanence, even for young people in the teenage years.

The dilemmas for those planning for adolescents who have been in the care system for some time or who have been in adoptive families that were now in difficulty, was whether they now needed a further chance at a family, and if so, would this be planned as a family for life. Prospective (Beek and Schofield, 2004a) and retrospective research (Schofield, 2003) has documented the significant role that a second, third, or fourth chance foster family at the age of 14, 15 or even 17 can play in some young peoples' lives. This role may include offering immediate support through to becoming grand-parents to their children – exactly the goals of permanence. This will not occur in all cases, but the fact that it is a possibility needs to be built into both single and dual systems.

Research has also emphasised the hope that adolescents placed in long-term/permanent foster care will find stability in the placements akin to the "objective permanence" dimension (Sinclair *et al*, 2005) i.e. providing a stable placement through childhood, but also providing back up and, if needed, accommodation after the age of 18. As Sinclair *et al*, found, many young people want to stay beyond 18 and longer in their foster families than they know is likely.

Use of age criteria in single and dual systems

Practitioners from local authorities with *single systems* identified that middle childhood and adolescent age groups had different needs and that there were different kinds of foster carers to meet those needs, but these could be encompassed within a single system.

We have got some young people who have been with carers for many years, so they were in place at nine or ten and are still with them now they are 16. Those young people are more or less part of the family but adoption wasn't an option. And there are carers who view these children as part of their family until such time as they move on and they tend to keep in touch as in a normal family situation . . . Other carers have come into fostering as a profession really and see it as a job they are doing in order to move a young person on, so they would take children long-term and they may be the ones who take the fourteen pluses, where there is a lot of home contact, so it is a different type of relationship. They are not trying to provide a replacement family for the child but what they are doing is looking after that child and enabling them to be safe but having contact with their own families. But that is still a long-term placement. (Fostering, single)

In this context again the concept of the foster family as a "replacement family", as opposed to an additional or supplementary family, is mentioned, as is the sense that the flexibility of the concepts of long-term and permanent care reflect not only the child's different needs but also the range of foster carers' motivation.

The questionnaire and interview data from practitioners in local authorities with the *dual system* suggested that their authority had attempted to formally differentiate between these two types of placements in terms of definitions (differences which were reinforced by different planning procedures in some dual authorities are discussed in the next chapter). But typically, long-term foster care was more commonly used when defining caring for adolescents, and permanent foster care as caring for children of middle childhood age.

Long-term foster care is much more likely to be for early adolescence, early mid adolescence, so you are looking at whether they are going to be there four, maybe five, years. Permanent foster care we would want really for anyone over the age of eight. Anyone under the age of eight we would want to be secured legally. Over the age of eight, we would also want legal security but if that wasn't possible, then we would look at permanence. (Fostering, dual)

This comment, and others like it from other dual authorities, suggests that in practice there is a likely age window of eight to perhaps 12 when permanent foster care would be an option, with long-term foster care reserved for teenagers.

Practitioners from authorities with dual systems often expected the two types of placements to fulfil the different needs of children from these age groups outlined above, such as family membership.

We wouldn't be encouraging children in long-term foster placements to make a very strong emotional attachment to their foster carers in the same way that we would be hoping that an emotional attachment would develop between children in permanent placement and their foster carers. (Fostering, dual)

Here we see explicitly the way in which attitudes and expectations about children's developmental needs, as discussed above, become enacted in planning policy, terminology and practice.

These links between age, expectations and placement terminology in single and dual authority systems were not, however, perceived by the practitioners to be rigid in all cases and many recognised that the level of contact, the quality of birth family relationships, the development of foster family membership and the length of the placement varied. Because a child was placed at a certain age did not automatically mean that they would follow the patterns outlined. Some staff from single system local authorities stated they were put off the dual system because children's needs could change over time and children of the same age may have different needs regarding these factors:

I would hope that it [a single system] was offering flexibility, because different children will have different needs. Some children may be 13, 14 years of age but they may need a family where they feel that they are going to become part of a family and remain part of a family. Whereas there may be other children who are 13, 14, depending on their personal circumstances, especially round either their family or their religion, ethnicity etc., where maybe they don't want to feel that involved with the family, but they need the permanence in terms of knowing where they were going home to every night. (Fostering, single)

A plan that is made for a child at the age of eight that says long-term foster care, may not still be an appropriate plan by the time they are 14. So while one would say long-term foster care means long-term until they become independent, that is not always the case and that would be reviewed within the usual statutory reviewing process. (LAC, single)

Such flexibility regarding teenagers might also be possible within a dual system where teenagers would also be long-term in most cases. Children of different ages, even within adolescence, might have different needs, but the fact that some need to be part of the family is acknowledged.

> *Well, I suppose it depends on when the child starts, because if you have a 15-year-old placed it is going to be a very different experience from having an 11-year-old placed. But at 15 I would like to think that they would still feel as though they are part of the family, but also there is going to have to be some kind of respect that they have another family that they still have attachments to. So I would expect them to join in and be there at meal times, but also be very aware that they have got a circle of friends that come with their birth family as well.*
> (IRO, dual)

But this flexibility around the needs of adolescents could only occur if practitioners were able to accommodate the possibility that the term "long-term" could mean permanence, i.e. lasting support and family membership, for some teenagers, and that other practices, such as LAC reviews, leaving care services and contact, would be managed to support a teenager who wanted a foster family to be a family into adulthood.

Age, need, systems – implications for practice

Although expectations of age and the length of the placement differ between agencies and models, what they have in common is a process of looking towards the end of the placement in defining the placement at the beginning. So the initial care plan, with its hopes and expectations for the placement to last till 18 or perhaps to continue into adult life, may be set at the outset, which could be when the child is as young as four or five (often in sibling groups if fostered) or as old as 14 or 15. This has important implications in terms of what actually does happen later, including the nature of "leaving care" services. But it also has major implications for foster carer recruitment, preparation and matching and in work with children and birth families during the placement. In adoption, there are assumptions made that by the very fact of a transfer of legal responsibility the adoptive parents have a model of what will happen at 18 – because it is what happens in ordinary families. For foster families, expectations that fostering a child will include certain expectations at 18 will not be so clear cut – and arguably this is one of the reasons that local authorities have sought through their systems of permanent and long-term foster care planning to give clearer signals from the beginning, and during a placement, to children, foster families and birth families that this placement will last.

Post-18 family care and membership appears to be a more explicit goal where local authorities have a model for foster care as permanence (whether this is *called* permanent or long-term foster care). But in other cases it is important that, even where lasting family membership is not in the plan at the outset, this would still be seen as something to value and support if the young person was deeply embedded in the foster family at that stage and the family was offering their care and concern into adulthood.

However, questions do arise about the expected "length" of those *long-term* foster care placements in *dual* system models and some placements were found as part of the long-term foster care range in *single* system models in which the expectation is *not* beyond 18 or into adult life, but is more likely to be until independence or leaving care (often at 16 or 17). Reasons for this more limited expectation are often expressed in terms of the age and needs of the child and the relationship with the birth family. But if we take it solely in terms of the anticipated length of placement, the first and most important issue is whether these placements should be thought of as "permanent". If such placements are considered alongside other permanence options, we find rather different points of comparison.

If long-term foster care till age 18 is compared with adoption in terms of *legal* expectations, then the gap is significant, since adoption is a legal transfer of parental responsibility for life and is expected to last for life. But if we compare foster care as a permanence option with special guardianship, increasingly seen as a positive permanence option, then this also legally lasts only until 18. In special guardianship, though, the length of time of the legal order is thought of as secondary to the nature of the commitment and the quality of the placement that should develop in what has become a more "normal" family because parental responsibility is held by the carers. This may suggest that the quality of the long-term foster carer placement could also offer something of permanence if expectations of the carers and the foster family were to be enhanced to reflect the plan. (Qualities and characteristics of foster carers as well as delegation of parental decision making are discussed below.)

Perhaps an equally important question is, if long-term foster care is *not* a permanence option in some local authorities i.e. does not clearly include a length of time as part of the family, and long-term fostered children do not have another permanence plan (e.g. to return home or be placed for adoption), how are those local authorities able to comply with the expectation that all looked after children have a permanence plan by the second review?

One complication, in particular, is whether a dual system agency which has permanent foster care placements can also have long-term foster care placements which are seen as permanent. But equally – do single system agencies have some placements that are more permanent than others? And does it help to have a single route called permanent foster care – which is currently the minority choice of model? All systems have within them the possibility of leaving out certain groups of children – mainly but not exclusively older children. Systems need to be inclusive, to work effectively and to make sense not only to professionals but also to the individual child, foster family and birth family.

Children accommodated under s20 (Children Act 1989)

Children who are accommodated under s20 (Children Act 1989) have been placed in care by agreement with their parents and parental responsibility remains with the parents and is not shared with the local authority. As stressed above, however, whatever the legal status of the child, the local authority as corporate parent is bound by the same duty of care under the Children Act 1989 s22, which is 'to safeguard the welfare of all looked after children'. The children are diverse in their histories and will have a range of needs, including, for some who do not have a plan for adoption or reunification, a need for a plan for permanence in foster care.

Almost all local authorities in this study had policies that included using long-term and/or permanent plans for accommodated children (96%, 79), as did nearly all IFPs (96%, 64). There were no statistical differences between systems, although there was a slight trend for fewer local authorities and IFPs with dual systems to use permanent foster care for accommodated children (LA 75%, IFP 78%). Even though almost all authorities and IFPs would *in principle* make long-term/permanence plans for children under s20, policy and attitudes towards making these plans and working with these placements varied across local authorities and between IFPs.

A number of the practitioners interviewed suggested that they only had a few children accommodated in long-term/permanent placements and such plans were not typical. However, the consensus would seem to be that where those with parental responsibility are co-operative and supportive, or at least make no attempt to disrupt the placement, then a placement under s20 can work as well, if not better, than a care order. In such cases there is often a direct process of negotiation between foster and birth parents.

We don't necessarily have that many children that are accommodated, to be honest, that are placed with long-term foster carers. The one or two that we do have, have really good relationships with parents so that again tends to work quite well – going back to the parent, going to school, activities with the parent, all that sort of thing. And you know the carers understand the decisions that parents are going to be making as well. (Fostering, single)

However, there are concerns that even where there is not a constructive partnership with parents, local authorities may sometimes feel unable to act in the child's best interests because they do not have parental responsibility.

This is not a satisfactory arrangement . . . The local authority has less say in arrangements and the foster carer is in a less secure position. (Questionnaire, LAC, single).

Some practitioners stated that if it was likely the child on s20 would not return home and would remain in foster care, they would seek a care order.

We have got a couple of children now who we want to keep where they are or to find permanence for and the parents have either gone AWOL or are being unhelpful, so we are actually applying for care orders. (Fostering, dual)

Almost all IFPs stated that they would provide long-term/permanent placements for accommodated children, indicating also that local authorities were prepared to fund these placements. Some IFP practitioners stated that the long-term/permanent placements could work well for accommodated children, with some similar themes about co-operation to those described by local authorities. One practitioner also mentioned that this was more common where teenagers were making many decisions for themselves:

Many long-term placements are for s20 teenagers and this seems to work well in reflecting the reality that the young people have a sense of autonomy and don't want restrictions forced on them. (Questionnaire, IFP)

One theme highlighted by IFP practitioners was that many accommodated children were in long-term/permanent placements with them which had happened "by default" rather than being planned as long-term/permanent in the first instance. The move from a short-term to long-term plan in the same placement is not necessarily a problem – indeed it is the most likely route to permanence in foster care. But the absence of a court sanctioned care plan sometimes led to drift and greater uncertainty, which in turn caused anxiety for carers and was problematic for IFPs in planning and obtaining a financial commitment for the long term. As in local authorities, some IFP practitioners felt that if it seemed likely that children were going to be looked after long term, a care order should be sought.

It's often by default. Problems often arise when birth families decide they want a child to return to them. This often does not last, but then we have the dilemma of whether we try and keep that placement open, and local authorities have to decide whether to fund this. I think it would be better to obtain a care order once a child has been accomodated for a certain period of time. (Questionnaire, IFP)

IFP practitioners also agreed with local authority workers that good practice made a difference and that long-term/permanent placements for accommodated children could 'work well if carers are supported properly' (Questionnaire IFP), were well planned and, in particular, had clear arrangements agreed for contact. In the absence of such arrangements, however:

[Section 20] can cause problems if all involved are not in agreement with the care plan and levels of contact with relatives need to be resolved from the start. (Questionnaire, IFP)

Unaccompanied asylum-seeking children

Unaccompanied asylum-seeking children are often accommodated under s20 Children Act 1989 because they are classed as "abandoned", one of the legal categories under s20.

We do work with a lot of unaccompanied asylum-seeking children who remain s20 where, for example, there may be nobody in the country who has PR for them. (Fostering, single)

There is also an anxiety for carers and social workers during a placement that young people will be deported when they reach 18 or go missing before 18 because of this risk.

We have UASC kids placed with carers and as they are approaching seventeen and a half, when they are supposed to get their decision about indefinite leave to remain, they just disappear and they go underground. (LAC, single)

Most study local authorities made, or would in principle make, long-term or permanent plans for unaccompanied asylum-seeking children (83%, 68). Significantly fewer local authorities with a dual system used permanent foster care (33%, 5) for this group compared to long-term foster care (67%, 12) or to local authorities with a single system (78%, 35)[9]. IFPs followed a similar pattern; however, there were generally significantly fewer IFPs than local authorities[10] which provided long-term and/or permanent placements for unaccompanied asylum-seeking children, with around two-thirds doing so in principle (63%, 41).

The majority of local authorities and IFPs had placed relatively few unaccompanied asylum-seeking children in long-term/permanent foster care, whereas certain authorities, depending on their location in the UK,

---

[9] $\chi2 = 10.0$, $df = 2$, $p<0.01$
[10] $\chi2 = 7.45$, $df = 2$, $p<0.01$

had placed larger numbers. Some practitioners commented in the questionnaire that these placements could work well: 'There are some examples of very good practice out there and good matches' (Fostering, single). Other practitioners suggested that unaccompanied asylum-seeking children were generally teenagers who often did not want to be cared for in foster care and preferred to live with their peers or, where possible, with friends or family.

> *The majority of our unaccompanied asylum-seeking children tend to be in their late teens upon arrival in the UK. We seek long-term or permanent placements appropriate to their needs . . . Over time the relevant team has also been keen to explore and pursue any available options for kinship placements, and a number of assessments are currently being undertaken. On occasion, some of our young people under 16 have been extremely reluctant or refused outright to be placed with foster carers. Where needed, appropriate legal advice has been sought. Despite encouragement to remain in placement, many of our young people are keen to move from foster care to semi-independent shared accommodation with their peers at 16.*
> (Questionnaire, fostering, dual)

Several practitioners commented that for younger unaccompanied asylum-seeking children their accommodated status was problematic. They were "abandoned" and yet the foster carer's parenting role appeared to be still very restricted. In order to overcome this, but within the limitations of knowledge of the birth parents' whereabouts, special guardianship orders had been taken out in some cases.

> *We have got two kids at the moment, who are unaccompanied asylum seekers with a matched carer. We have struggled to trace birth mothers for both of them and we are actually looking at permanence with the foster carer but we are looking at it via a SGO with us giving her a payment almost equivalent to her fostering allowance. Because then if the birth mothers ever do surface and actually want to resume care of their children, they can go to court and ask for the SGO to be overturned whereas if they are adopted that is a real struggle.* (LAC, single)

It seems that local authorities and the independent sector are taking the needs of unaccompanied asylum-seeking children for permanence seriously within their different systems. But they are having to manage care planning in circumstances which include a range of legal uncertainties regarding the exercise of parental responsibility and regarding immigration status – as well as a range of stressful and challenging circumstances of the young people themselves (Wade *et al*, 2006; Kohli and Mitchell, 2007).

Family and friends placements

Local authorities in the study varied in the extent to which family and friends placements followed similar definitions and patterns to unrelated carers in different systems. Almost two-thirds of local authorities would classify them as either long-term or permanent foster placements, with no clear pattern between single and dual systems. Other local authorities did not appear to categorise them in this way, but simply referred to them as family or friends carers, kinship carers or family network carers regardless of plan. However, nearly all practitioners stated that if a child could not return home, the next best option would be for them to remain with family or friends: 'You have got to make sure that all family members have been considered' (Fostering, single).

Many practitioners commented that family and friends carers did 'not respond well to professional involvement' (Questionnaire, fostering, single), and that although carers needed support, they did not feel that they should be thought of in the same way as "mainstream" long-term/permanent carers.

I don't really think they should be foster carers, you know. I think there should be a different status for them altogether really. I am not saying they shouldn't have checks and they shouldn't have to have some quite stringent assessments and if they wanted to access services like training and things because they looked after somebody else's child that should be available to them. But I am not sure if you are somebody's grandparent, you want to be the foster parent. (Fostering, single)

Many commented that they encouraged family and friends carers to take out special guardianship orders and had had some success, especially as they could often manage contact well and would benefit from the extra parental responsibility.

We are encouraging carers to apply for SGOs where we have got kids placed, say, with extended family, the extended family is on placement with parent regs and they have been there long term and the placement is stable. There is maybe not a need for us to be involved. (LAC, single)

Special guardianship was also accepted as a more suitable alternative to adoption because of the shared parental responsibility, allowing the child to retain an identity linked to the birth family:

We would be considering special guardianship . . . rather than adoption . . . It allows the child to retain their family identity, both in terms of their birth parents who won't be their carers, but also recognising the fact that this is a member of their extended family and there will still be linkage with birth parents. So they won't have the parental responsibility removed, but the family member caring for the child on a permanent basis will also have parental responsibility and will be able to exercise it to the exclusion of the parents if necessary. It makes for a more constructive extended family placement, because there is not the resentment if there is, you know, the exclusivity of an adoption order. (LAC, single)

Although the policy for most local authorities was to include family and friends foster placements as an appropriate *permanence* plan within routes common to other foster placements, there was an acknowledgement that these were not the same as other foster placements and that attempts needed to be made to tailor their systems, including access to support for special guardianship applications, in ways that were more appropriate to these rather different family circumstances (see also discussion of special guardianship, Chapter 8).

Care planning systems and stability performance indicators

The relationship between single and dual systems and government performance indicators for long-term stability was checked for 2005–6 (Department for Education and Skills, 2007b).

Using the D35 indicator, on average, 50 per cent (range 34–64%) of all children from our English study authorities who had been looked after continuously for at least four years had been in their foster placement for the last two years. These figures were very similar to the total figures for all England local authorities on this indicator, which gave an average of 51 per cent (range 30–68%).

Using the D78 performance indicator, on average, 63 per cent (range 45–80%) of all children from our English study authorities who had been looked after continuously for at least two-and-a-half years had been in the same placement for at least two years or had been placed for adoption. Here too the figures were very similar to the total figures for all England local authorities, which gave an average of 65 per cent (range 45–90%).

These indicators pick up rather different aspects of long-term stability and the D35 indicator has now been discontinued in favour of the D78. Although both indicators have their limitations, the wide range of local authority performance on both does raise some important questions about differences in corporate parenting and planning systems and practice. But most important for our purposes was the fact that on these measures there were no significant differences in our study between local authorities with single and dual systems for care planning for permanence in foster care.

Whatever factors are affecting long-term stability, at least as measured by these indicators, it does not appear to be the systems themselves, but is likely to have more to do with the operation of the systems, the quality of planning and practice in each authority – and the quality of foster placements, a point emphasised by Sinclair *et al* (2007, p. 305).

4 Care planning for children

Identifying different care planning systems and their implications for children and families has always proved a challenge for researchers (Lowe and Murch *et al*, 2002), especially where the placement goals are outcomes that may be years away from the processes and meetings that launched the placement. Long-term outcomes are difficult to link to the details of the initial planning system and it is probably impossible to reliably trace specific outcomes to different procedural systems as opposed to other factors e.g. degree of difficulty presented by the child, quality of foster carers or social work practice. However, it is likely that the nature and quality of care planning in individual cases will certainly *contribute* to outcomes in the short, medium and long-term. The decisions to place a child for adoption or foster care, to match a child in this particular new placement and to promote or end birth family contact will all be part of care planning and will, in interaction with other factors, make a difference to children's happiness and well-being. Making decisions and plans for children in care that increase the likelihood of an upward spiral of stability, educational success, secure relationships and a sense of belonging, rather than a downward spiral of repeated moves, school failure, problematic relationships and uncertain family identities remains a major responsibility for those who devise and operationalise planning systems.

Local authorities are expected to organise their services to ensure that children's plans are made and reviewed appropriately, so it is not surprising to find from this study that most local authorities put a great deal of thought, effort and, in many cases, significant financial resources into their care planning systems. Because of the lack of research and national concerns about outcomes, it is perhaps also not surprising that although some authorities were confident that their established systems were working well, others in the study were in the position of having just reorganised their planning as well as social work delivery systems or were just about to reorganise them.

When local authorities are reviewing their own systems and planning new ones, in this area of practice as in many others, there is a very limited collaborative culture or framework to enable them to learn from other local authorities – although some do consult with comparator authorities. From our study it was evident that some local authorities were, for example, going from single to dual systems, without even knowing that a neighbouring authority was currently moving in the opposite direction. Until this study, there have been no widely available even *descriptive* accounts of practice in a cross-section of other local authorities that could be used as possible models – and there is still the need for more research on *effectiveness*.

Panels and meetings for best interests and matching recommendations

Having looked in some detail in the previous chapter at the definitions and expectations of long-term and permanent foster care in different models, it is important to think about which planning pathways are available to these local authorities to support these different systems. One of the reasons for the focus on the role of panels was to investigate not only the level and type of scrutiny of assessment documentation and care plans, but to consider comparisons with and lessons that could be learned from adoption practice. In particular, the best interests decision and the match between the child and the carer must be seen as central to any successful care plan.

There are a number of different panels and meetings that feature in combination. Some will be required by statute, regulation and guidance, while others are determined by local policy and practice.

- Panels/meetings that are *statutory* and used according to regulation and in broadly similar ways by all local authorities e.g. looked after children reviews chaired by independent reviewing officers.
- Panels that are *statutory*, with some required activities and regulated membership, but used for *varied purposes* in relation to permanence in foster care e.g. fostering panels, adoption panels.
- Panels/meetings that are *almost universal but have no statutory force* or regulated activities or membership e.g. planning meetings.

- Panels that have *the same names but very different status and functions* in different authorities e.g. a "permanency panel" may be the local name for a statutory adoption panel which may or may not include long-term or permanent foster care decisions OR it may be a social services panel that meets at intervals to monitor children for whom a permanence plan is needed.
- Panels that are *common, but not universal*, and may only be used in certain cases e.g. resource panels used for IFP, residential and out of county placements or for placements in specialist schemes that are in house.
- Local panels that are *named and constituted locally and used for particular purposes* e.g. a "children's panel", used to manage and monitor all children in the care system, including those who may be subject to a plan for long-term and permanent foster care OR a long-term fostering panel, through which all plans and matches for long-term fostering must pass before going to the fostering panel.

A number of these meetings and panels do not have the right to make *final decisions* about care plans, best interests, approval of carers and matching. Even fostering panels and adoption panels make *recommendations*. Thus, the role of *agency decision makers* is very important. These are usually senior managers, with some agencies having separate decision makers for adoption and fostering whereas others combine these roles. They have to consider the documentation and arguments put by the panels before either asking for more information or making the decision.

The care planning routes

There are a series of decisions that need to be made when formulating a care plan. First is the decision as to whether the child's need for permanence will be best met in a foster family – so *a best interests decision* needs to be made following appropriate assessment. The process of arriving at the decision to pursue a plan for long-term or permanent foster care in relation to a particular child is most likely to start informally in discussions between the child and family social worker and their supervisor or team manager, once it is recognised that a child needs a plan for permanence outside of the birth parents' care.

Depending on the timing of such discussions – and whether the case is in court proceedings or not – the options will be put to a planning meeting or a LAC review or both. Because the LAC review is asked to review plans rather than make them, the role of these two meetings may overlap, since the recommendation to consider a permanence in foster care plan may emerge from a LAC review of another permanence plan (e.g. to return the child home or to place for adoption) that it has not been possible to implement. Alternatively, the care plan may emerge following an assessment of a child yet to be subject of a plan, be confirmed at a planning meeting and then considered as part of a LAC review. So the plan may start at a planning meeting or LAC review, then proceed via the other meeting or move up to a further level in the system (resource panel, fostering panel, adoption and permanence panel) for further consideration. The composition of these meetings and panels is important as they may include any combination of social worker and other professionals and lay representatives. But only certain meetings, often at the earlier stages, will automatically include foster carers, birth parents and other relatives – or the child.

This study has shown that during this process (perhaps at an early stage or between a planning meeting and a formal submission to a fostering panel) some agencies send care plans on each case for scrutiny and quality control by individual permanence or placement managers or to a meeting or panel that oversees all children's cases when decisions are being made about how best to achieve permanence. These may have different names e.g. permanency planning meeting or children's panel. There are also some specific panels for monitoring long-term fostering decisions (see below for further discussion of these processes).

Where the *court* is involved because a child is in care or adoption proceedings, complex parallel systems of care planning will be operating within the court and within the local authority. An interview with an IRO in the study reported very helpfully on how the assessment, recommendation, decision making and care planning in each child's case flowed in and out of these parallel systems. Not only were decisions made in one place being checked, considered or reconsidered in another, information in the form of different assessment documentation was also presented in one place or another without always being shared. The role of document-ation in different local authority systems is discussed below. But it is important to bear in mind that assessments in the form of statements for court that contribute to the court's care planning may not be available in other decision-making forums. Similarly, paperwork and direct reporting e.g. the views of birth relatives or current foster carers, which were available at a LAC review, may not have been available to the court. Much of this is determined by local custom and practice, with this particular IRO commenting that she was copied into documents sent to the adoption panel but not to the fostering panel.

Secondly, a *suitable foster family* needs to be *identified* or *recruited* and *approved* as long-term or permanent carers. Where a child is in a foster placement with approved short-term carers who are willing to offer a long-term home, the carers and the family will need reassessment prior to the new approval. Where carers new to either the agency and/ or to the child are being considered, they too need to be assessed and then approved.

In this area of decision making, there is less room for locally varied systems, as in both single and dual systems it is likely that approval will be made at the fostering panel. The only exception apparent in the study were the small number of authorities who have a joint panel for adoption and permanence in foster care, which meets the regulations for both adoption and fostering and which might approve permanent or long-term foster carers for this role.

Thirdly, a *matching decision* needs to be made, in which the child's needs in the short, medium and longer term are matched to the carers' and family's capacity to meet those needs into the future. Here, as with best interests decisions, there is no specific regulation or guidance (unlike in adoption) and so the decision-making forum and the basis on which the matching decisions are made will depend on local variation both in use of panels and assessment proforma.

Age and use of meetings or panels

Before looking at the study findings in more detail, it is important to note that although most local authorities used particular panels for particular categories of placement, a proportion of single system local authorities (18%) used *two different panels* to make recommendations for different children within the same category (long-term or permanent). The interview data suggested that local authorities who used more than one panel for a particular category based their panel choice on the *age* of the child, with recommendations regarding children in middle childhood typically brought to the permanence panel or adoption and permanence panel, and recommendations regarding adolescents being brought to the fostering panel.

> *All matching for children of 12 and under will go via the adoption and permanency planning panel and matching for 12 pluses will go via the fostering panel.* (Fostering, single)

One major reason for this was said to be that more adolescent placements were temporary placements which were being changed to long-term and it was felt that, as panels were extremely busy, the younger children who were going to stay in the system longer should be prioritised. But both routes could lead to a permanent foster care plan regardless of age, as in this single/permanent local authority.

> *We have two ways of matching for permanent foster care, one for under 14 and one for over 14. At 14 plus it doesn't go to panel it goes to our Head of Quality Assurance ... Mainly because of two issues: one is a capacity issue, because if all of the cases to match for permanence went to panel, panel would be sitting three days a week. Well, maybe not three days a week, but certainly ... it meets once a month at the moment and it would need to do a lot more than that. The other issue is that often the young person has been with that carer for a long, long time and a lot of the assessment and matching are evident within the whole review process.* (LAC, single)

This age distinction in *planning procedure* in some *single system* authorities is consistent with the detailed earlier discussion about age and expectations in terms of how placements were *defined*. As with definitions, age-related procedures for permanent foster care in authorities with the *dual system* were also designed to distinguish it from long-term foster care. Some authorities with the dual system referred to adolescent placements routinely as long-term and the placements of younger children taken to panel as permanent.

Although this age distinction has already emerged from the discussion of definitions, this use of different panels for children of different ages, confirms the fact that age, with the associated attitudes and expectations about the nature of new family relationships, may often be more important in terms of planning than whether there is a single or dual system or whether the placement is called long-term or permanent.

Children remaining with current carers – best interests and matching

Other research (Schofield *et al*, 2000, 2007) has identified that in some agencies there may be differences in the way in which decisions are made at these two stages (best interests and match) for children remaining with current carers and those moving to new carers. Questions were therefore asked separately for each route and did indeed find some variations. Some but not all of these variations were linked to the differences between single and dual models of long-term and permanent foster care.

In the analysis of the care planning data from the study, it seemed important to clarify the type of panel or scrutiny that was used for children who remained with current carers in comparison to those who moved to new carers. It was not possible for local authorities to put figures on these two groups, but social workers suggested that the majority of plans were built on current placements and that best interests decisions and matching were often conducted with the current placement in mind. (For convenience, the term "decisions" is used, with the caveat that these need in many cases to be thought of as recommendations to be later confirmed or questioned by the agency decision maker.)

The pattern of meeting and panel use does not necessarily reflect the different single and dual models. Nevertheless, overall permanent foster care cases in dual system authorities are least likely to have the *best interests* decision made at the LAC review and more likely to have it made at a permanence panel or an adoption and permanence panel. However, single system authorities were less likely to have the decision made at the

LAC review and more likely to have it made at an adoption and permanence panel than long-term in dual systems. Such distinctions are compatible with the distinction between permanent and long-term in the dual systems, but also the differences between how long-term is perceived in those authorities for whom it is their permanence route.

The most common route in all local authorities was that the *best interests* decisions for children to remain with current carers would be made at the *fostering panel*. However, it seems unlikely that local authorities actually take best interests decisions to fostering panels separately from the matching decision. It seems more likely that at the point of the matching decision, the best interests decision for the child and the match with the named carers are made at the same time. This seems particularly likely where children are to be matched with current carers and the role of the panel is to approve the carer as a long-term or permanent carer for this particular child.

Although dual system authorities distinguished between long-term and permanent placement plans, only 39 per cent (9) used different panels (or meetings) for *matching* children with their current carer for long-term or for permanent foster care. Long-term foster care matching decisions are more likely to be made at meetings such as the LAC review or planning meeting without later scrutiny by statutory panels (see Figure 4.1 overleaf). More dual system authorities use an adoption and permanence panel (21%, 5) for matching permanent foster placements than use it for long-term fostering (8%, 2). Use of adoption panels for foster care is generally limited. The largest number of cases (50–63%) across all groups are matched with current carers at the fostering panel.

Children moving to new carers – best interests and matching

Best interests recommendations for children going to foster carers new to them were made at the level of the LAC review for just over a quarter of single system study local authorities and for long-term foster care in the dual system. Whereas for permanent foster care, a quarter of authorities used the adoption panel and less than five per cent used a LAC review.

In single systems, more use is made of the fostering panel for long-term foster care than in dual authorities, where more took this decision to

Figure 4.1

Percentage of authorities which used each meeting or panel for the matching recommendation for current placements in each system (NB Two panel system = different panels for different age children)

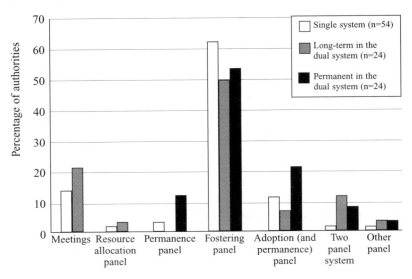

resource panels. It is not clear the extent to which resource panels were involved because an IFP placement might need a funding agreement or whether the panel was also needed to monitor the resources of their own fostering service – for example, making a long-term match with a skilled task-centred carer has implications for the availability of task-centred placements.

The pattern of panel use for *matching* in new placements reflects to some extent the distinctions being made between long-term and permanent foster care and between models (Figure 4.2). Dual authorities were more likely to use the LAC review for the match for long-term foster care than for their permanent foster care placements or single authorities. However, as for matches with current carers, the largest proportion of authorities (43–55%) in both systems matched children with new carers at the fostering panel. Resource panels seemed to be used more for long-term fostering in the dual authorities, but this may be because these placements were more often teenagers and perhaps placements were more costly.

Use of the adoption and permanence panel was more common for matching new permanent foster care placements in dual systems (33%, 7) than in single systems (15%, 8) – with no long-term foster care matches in dual system authorities receiving this type of scrutiny. Numbers again are small in each category, which suggests that even in authorities for which long-term is a permanence option or which choose to have a permanent foster care option, most decision making stays with the fostering panel or LAC review and does not approach the adoption arena.

Half (50%, 10) of dual system local authorities used a different panel for matching with a new carer in long-term and permanent foster placements; however, the panel used most for the match by *all* systems was the fostering panel (42–55%).

Figure 4.2

The percentage of authorities which used each meeting or panel for the matching recommendation for new placements in each system

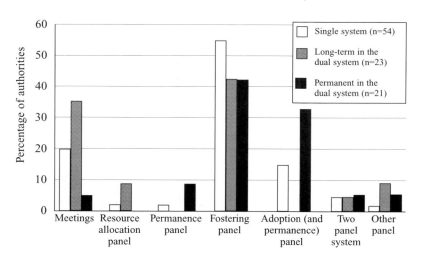

Family and friends placements

There was varying quality of data regarding planning for family and friends placements, as a number of local authorities had developed different terminologies and systems to manage those placements that were informal, those that became approved carers and those for whom this was expected to be a temporary stage on the way to a residence or special guardianship order.

Local authorities indicated on the questionnaire that the best interests decision for children placed with family and friends carers could be made at various levels, including the fostering panel, but it seemed unlikely that, as with unrelated carers, best interests decisions for these placements were being made separately from the matching process with a specific family.

Some distinctions were being made between long-term and permanent family and friends carers, but less than a sixth (16%, 3) of dual system

Figure 4.3

The percentage of authorities which used each meeting or panel for the matching recommendation for family and friends placements in each system

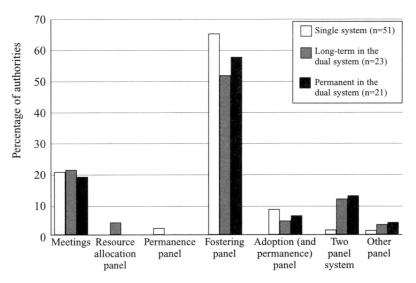

authorities used different panels to match children with a family and friends carer for long-term or for permanent foster placements (see Figure 4.3). The fostering panel was used most for the match, with well over half of authorities using it, as shown by Figure 4.3. Planning meetings and LAC reviews were used by around a fifth; however, adoption and permanence panels/permanence panels were used by very few authorities. This may be because family and friends placements are seen as more appropriately remaining with fostering rather than adoption practice.

Practitioner views of different meetings, panels and planning systems

Permanency planning meetings and Looked after Children (LAC) reviews

The meeting identified by many of the practitioners as being the start of planning a long-term/permanent placement was the *permanency planning* meeting, sometimes called a *referral* meeting. This meeting normally occurred after the child had been looked after for three months in order to have a permanence plan in place, as required, for the second *LAC review* at four months. This was a fairly typical account.

> *Within a three-month period we would have what we call a permanency planning meeting and following on from that permanency planning meeting there would be regular reviews. So fairly early on we would be looking at what the options are, whether or not the child could be reunited with the birth family as part of the care plan or whether the child needed to move on to a more permanent placement, which might be adoption, or whether it may need to go into longer-term foster care. So those are the options that we would all look at under the permanency planning meetings and their reviews.* (Fostering, dual)

The key point here is that the plan at this stage was often likely, pending further assessment or court decisions, to be a "twin track" or "parallel" plan of return home or permanent family placement in adoption or foster care, a process monitored by the Chair of the LAC review, the independent reviewing officer (IRO).

The first review takes place within 28 days, and quite often a care plan is undetermined. But it's the second review when we have to put down on the LAC Review form . . . review of arrangements, what the care plan is, even if it's twin tracking. Quite often it could be adoption, long-term care or return home. But at a very early stage we have to have the basis of a long-term plan . . . (IRO, dual)

A number of authorities stated that their permanency planning had not been sufficiently robust in the past and having only recently implemented special permanency planning meetings, they were trying to undertake them for all the children in their care.

We are literally going through and finding out which cases have and haven't had plans. We are going very systematically through cases. Social workers are presenting those cases and out of that comes a confirmed plan. The permanency meeting currently is fortnightly to make sure we get through the backlog properly, but thereafter it is likely to be probably about six-weekly. (LAC, single).

One local authority stated that permanency planning meetings happened for children who were likely to be suitable for adoption, but not children who were more likely to be placed in foster care.

It happens sometimes in adoption, but rarely in fostering situations where you have a formal care planning kind of meeting, a formal permanence planning meeting where all the relevant people are present, and then come up with that child's care plan in a formal way. (Fostering, single)

In this situation such a meeting has a role in relation to selected individual cases but less of a role in monitoring the system – in contrast to the previous quotation.

Fostering panels

As is clear from the survey findings discussed above, the fostering panel was the panel most commonly used for matching decisions by most authorities for both permanent and long-term placements. On the whole, both practitioners who took cases to the panel and those who sat on or chaired fostering panels felt that the panel had the right level of expertise to make decisions about long-term/permanent cases.

The fostering panels obviously have a really good understanding about fostering. We have got six panels in [local authority] and they are very experienced now at doing long-term linking. They are quite well established and have a really good, developed understanding of what they are being asked to do and they are very good at quality assurance, looking at what is best for the young person. So I think it is a really effective way of using them. (Fostering, single)

However, some felt that a permanency panel would be more appropriate because it had a higher level of expertise.

My only comment would be that I think that what my authority lacks is a forum which has a high degree of specialism and understanding of the research involved in permanency planning. So I think that is an absolutely essential part of any kind of permanency planning, whether it be long-term fostering or anything else. I think that probably a forum with that expertise would be in a better position. So a permanency panel would be better, because you would develop that expertise. (LAC, single)

This view came from a practitioner in the same agency as quoted immediately above, showing that there is some debate even within agencies – and that possibly there might be differences of opinion between the fostering and the LAC services.

Whatever questions were raised about the role and expertise of the fostering panel, several practitioners and managers from authorities who relied only on LAC reviews or planning meetings for long-term and permanent foster care best interests and matching decisions expressed a wish for this higher and more independent level of scrutiny.

My own personal view, rather than the authority's view, would be that we need to formalise the permanence system further, actually, and I would like to see the fostering panel involved in recommending the match, but at the moment that isn't happening. I would like to see it happening as a way of providing external scrutiny of the matching process. (Fostering, dual)

Practitioners who wanted the fostering panel to become routinely involved felt that it might prevent disruption of placements in the future by offering this extra level of scrutiny.

I think it is obviously important to have the LAC review and decisions confirmed there because it gives everybody a greater message of the importance of this being a permanent arrangement. It actually also brings more scrutiny to the matching process. But I think the fostering panel could advise in terms of there may be something that we have missed. That is certainly what they did in the local authority where I used to work and we also were able successfully to have the child come to the panel and they heard a very good message. (Fostering, single)

Many practitioners commented that where the child was to remain with the same carer the match should still be taken to a panel.

If we put somebody somewhere short term and that carer said we will keep them permanently, then we would plan to do it properly and it would all go to the panel. They would never just sit there from the age of seven till eighteen, not going through the process. (Fostering, single)

The use of fostering panels for so much of the decision making regarding best interests and matching for permanence in foster care does, however, raise some important questions about the role, expertise and training of fostering panels. These questions were discussed in some of the interviews. Although it is not new for fostering panels to approve both kinship and unrelated foster carers as long-term carers for a named child – and so have to read and review evidence on the child's developmental and other needs – the focus has tended to be on ensuring that this carer can meet the particular child's needs. This is not quite the same as also considering whether, for example, foster care rather than other options would be in the child's best interests as a permanence option or coming to conclusions about the kind of specialised medical or psychiatric support that may be needed to ensure the matched placement will work in practice.

The increasing role of fostering panels in agreeing a best interests decision and matching children with carers was put to panel Chairs and others. There was a general view that the panels worked well – but in the discussion it nevertheless seemed that the focus and expertise of fostering panels were more clearly centred on the carer than on the child. The developing use of fostering panels in this area certainly needs to be considered in the training, support and even membership of panels. Some panels, for example, have a full medical assessment of the child and a medical adviser present, but others do not. (Further discussion of documentation considered by panels is provided below.) Agencies clearly have a choice as to who is making the permanence decisions, but whether this is a planning meeting, a fostering panel or an adoption and permanence panel, members need to receive the appropriate document-ation and have the relevant knowledge and expertise to use and evaluate it as a basis for decisions.

Adoption and permanence panels or permanence panels

The questionnaire data showed that a small proportion of study local authorities used an adoption and permanence panel or a permanence panel constituted to act in adoption as well as fostering cases. In the interview sample, practitioners whose authorities took long-term/permanent cases to the adoption and permanence panel or the permanence panel stated that they did so because it had the right level of expertise to make decisions about children's long-term future.

[Local authority] doesn't have the resources to create another panel so therefore the adoption and permanence panel considers the matches for permanence. I think because of the nature of the panel and its make up and the different backgrounds of its members, it focuses very much on the long term, the future of the child and how they can achieve stability and permanency, whether it be through adoption or long-term fostering. So, therefore, we feel that it is right that those matches come to our panel rather than a fostering panel which deals with approvals of temporary carers. So, you know, we are very happy

that at [local authority] matches for permanency come to our panel and not to the fostering panel. (Panel Chair, single)

A theme which many practitioners highlighted as a reason for using the adoption and permanence panel or the permanence panel was that by taking cases to the panel it conveyed a message to carer, birth parents and practitioners that the placement was expected to last until adulthood and required extra commitment.

I think that is one of the reasons that [local authority] has recently brought this in. We now bring permanent matches to adoption and permanency panel because we felt it was important in a number of areas. One is that I think it reinforces the message, if you like, to some birth parents that this is a permanent alternative placement for your child. I think it brings it into sharp focus to permanent foster carers because obviously there is an inbuilt matching process and they are part and parcel of that. And they can come to panel, so again that raises the profile of it and for the child as well. (Fostering, dual)

A number of practitioners whose authorities used the fostering panel stated that they felt the permanence panel or an adoption and permanence panel was a more appropriate place for recommendations about long-term/permanent foster care and would prefer to be moving towards it in their authority.

I am not quite convinced that [local authority] has its panel system right, because I would make it a permanence panel rather than an adoption panel. But in [local authority], the fostering panel considers all fostering and the adoption panel considers any of those children for whom the social worker, and then usually a departmental meeting, has agreed that adoption is the right plan. I personally would like permanent fostering to go much more down the adoption route and that is how I would do it. (IRO, dual)

One of the reasons for not taking long-term/permanent cases to the adoption and permanence panel, even where this had previously been the case, was because of capacity difficulties. As some agencies were moving towards this option, others were moving away from it.

Between 2003 and 2005 all the permanence matches and approval of foster carers went to the adoption and permanence panel, but then our panel could not cope with the volume of work. (Fostering, single)

The use of the adoption or adoption and permanence panel for permanence in foster care is likely to need considerable investment of resources. Whether this is the right route, compared to developing the role (and expertise?) of fostering panels as some have done, requires some careful analysis. This study cannot offer a view on the relative merits of these alternatives, but the composition, skills, training and documentation used by both panels is likely to need to be adapted in the light of a move to include best interests and matching in the full range of long-term and permanent fostering.

Other systems and panels for promoting and monitoring care planning for permanence in foster care

Alongside these meetings and panels that make decisions about named children, a number of local authorities have developed systems for promoting and monitoring their permanency planning for all their children in care. Most local authorities have individual staff members who monitor the LAC population to some degree. These are sometimes senior managers, with titles such as corporate parenting manager, or middle managers, team leaders or practitioner experts, such as senior practitioners for permanence or long-term fostering. These people play key roles in monitoring the system and tracking individual children, often as well as providing expertise to social work colleagues and others, such as legal advisers and courts.

We do have a permanency officer whose job it is to make sure that these matters are progressed. He has been very helpful. His role is to join with the social worker and the supervising social worker and ensure that matters are progressed to some form of permanency outcome, if that is appropriate. (LAC, single)

In one of the large single system study authorities using long-term foster care, there was very active management of the system through two workers who between them not only monitored the children who were in need of a long-term foster placement, but also held special long-term foster care planning meetings. They advised the social worker in preparing the documentation, met the foster carer and made sure that assessment documentation going to the fostering panel was up to standard.

It was clear from the survey and the interviews that the work of monitoring looked after children has been significantly facilitated in recent years by the availability of more detailed and more widely available administrative data on children in care e.g. age, gender, reasons for being in care, legal status, placements and moves. The UK has some of the best administrative data in the developed world (Thoburn, 2007; Thoburn, 2008). The availability of these data, in some agencies updated constantly or in monthly reports rather than through an annual reporting system, is one of the positive consequences of a performance management culture in children's services.

However, the Department for Children, Schools and Families (DCSF) performance indicators do not make reference to children's plans (see Schofield *et al*, 2007 for wider discussion of this issue). Thus data are not easily available on this very important element in the system and local authorities trying to ensure that all children do have permanence plans and that no-one is drifting have had to put a great deal of work into finding ways of recording plans in a more transparent and accessible way.

In addition to the existence of key individuals monitoring the system, there were a range of meetings and panels that contributed to this work. Some of the "permanency planning meetings" mentioned above had the role of monitoring the system as well as or instead of planning for individual children. It was not clear the extent to which resource panels also monitored the system as well as making decisions about placements. In most authorities that use them, resource panels become involved when placement decisions have financial implications and expenditure needs to be authorised – either in terms of additional resources for local authority carers or to fund an IFP or residential placement. This was seen as a further level of scrutiny – but in terms of weighing an assessment of the child's needs against the relative costs of different placements. As with fostering and adoption panels, the composition and training of these panels may also raise some issues in terms of expertise in children's developmental needs and the potential ability of foster carers to offer permanence.

One local authority reported on their "Children's Panel". This was additional to the LAC reviews and other statutory panels and had the goal of ensuring that each child had a plan for permanency by monitoring plans of all looked after children. All children's cases would come to this panel, regardless of their care arrangements (i.e. including children in residential care) if it was flagged up that they did not have a permanence plan on the system or the plan was not yet implemented.

The Children's Panel has a clear role in progressing the care plans of looked after children. They would be involved at the very beginning of the child's entrance into the care system and they regularly review the progress of the permanency plan. It is to avoid drift and delay. They are also responsible for the endorsement of twin track and parallel planning. The primary purpose is to ensure the improvement and the quality of life of looked after children and make sure appropriate permanency arrangements are in place for them. They are multi-agency, they have a core membership, they work in line with all the current local authority procedures and there is a very clear agenda and plan for them for what they should be doing in terms of progressing permanency for children. What has happened as a result of that is that their role has been extended slightly to ensure quality assurance and performance indicators around permanency. It works well is my understanding. They track the progress of permanency planning for children...and because they are the operational heads as well, they can then go back to the operational managers and say 'I have not had papers on..', you know, 'This hasn't been presented to children's panel, why?' (Fostering, dual)

It is clear that local authority practice in monitoring their care population in terms of their plans is very varied, mainly because this is not data linked to performance indicators or required to be aggregated and submitted to the DCSF. But these systems seem promising and do need to be looked at in more detail so that a range of innovative good practice can be identified and shared with other authorities.

Documentation used for best interests and matching decisions

The type and quality of documentation used by local authorities for assessing children and carers and making the match is central to any attempt to identify good practice and this varied considerably between authorities. In this area of practice, there did not seem to be any pattern of difference between single and dual systems (as shown in Table 4.1.).

Nearly all authorities used a social work report and care plan for the best interests recommendation/decision and a social work report for the matching recommendation and decision. These documents were used by most of the authorities at all panels and meetings, but the content and structure of the social work report and the care plan was acknowledged to vary in content and quality. Almost all local authorities used a carer's report, generally an updated BAAF Form F, for the approval and the match. However, this was mostly presented when fostering or adoption panels were involved, suggesting that there could be a lesser amount of information available in those cases remaining at the LAC review level.

The *quality* of the assessment of child and carer would, of course, not necessarily follow from the choice of documentation. More formal structures might produce different kinds of information and assessments, but it would be the skill and knowledge base of the practitioner that would be making a difference to quality, accuracy and usefulness. As important, therefore, was the quality assurance approach. In one authority the long-term foster care co-ordinators would return reports to social workers if they did not adequately cover the information or appropriately present the professional judgements required and in others team managers were active in this role.

Between 55 per cent and 74 per cent (depending on the model) of authorities used full medical reports. The medical report was used slightly less by authorities for best interests and matching in a long-term place-ment in dual system compared to the long-term single system or perman-ent placements in the dual system. This may be expected, as long-term in the dual system often referred to older children whose matching took place within the LAC review and planning system. Indeed, medical reports were used by nearly all authorities who stated they used the adoption and permanence panel and the majority of authorities who used the fostering panel. This compared with around a third of authorities who made decisions at reviews and internal meetings. School reports appeared to be used by almost two-thirds of local authorities for the best interests recommendation, but were only used by around 50 per cent for the match.

The adoption and permanence panel required the highest level of documentation with over 80 per cent of local authorities who used this panel for the match requiring all of the documentation listed below. Although around three-quarters of local authorities who used the fostering panel required a social work report, carers' report and matching report, only around half of them required a child's permanence report (CPR).

Table 4.1
Documentation used for the best interests and the matching decisions

Documentation	Recommendation	Single (BI n = 51, M n = 49)	Long-term dual (n = 20)	Permanent dual (n = 20)
Social work report	Best interests	94%	95%	100%
	Match	83%	80%	85%
Care plan	Best interests	92%	90%	95%
	Match	n/a	n/a	n/a
Carers' report	Best interests	82%	80%	85%
	Match	78%	70%	85%
Permanence report	Best interests	55%	45%	50%
	Match	65%	35%	55%
Matching report	Best interests	n/a	n/a	n/a
	Match	84%	60%	75%
Full medical report	Best interests	69%	55%	74%
	Match	63%	45%	60%
School report	Best interests	71%	70%	65%
	Match	57%	40%	45%

However, this is still fairly high considering the CPR was originally designed to be used for adoption recommendations at an adoption panel.

The use of the child's permanence report in long-term and permanent foster care

The child's permanence report (Form CPR) is a document produced by BAAF for assessing the child in relation to achieving an appropriate best interests decision for permanence and a good match.

The CPR appeared to be used by slightly fewer authorities when matching a long-term placement in the dual system. This difference may reflect the perceived function of the placements and the fact that older children were generally less likely to have a permanence report. In some local authorities, use of the CPR depended explicitly on the age of the child. It would be used with children of middle childhood, but not usually adolescents. This was often linked to those cases being brought to a specific panel. Similarly, planning a permanent foster placement in the dual system was more likely to involve a child's permanence report. In this example, the distinction is linked to age and panel.

We are slightly more flexible in relation to the paperwork for matching at a fostering panel as opposed to adoption panel, so we don't insist on a child's permanence report for the over-12s going to fostering panel. We haven't entirely replicated the adoption system in terms of the child's permanence report, but for any cases being presented to the adoption and permanence panel, if they are for under-12s, we would expect there to be the child's permanence report and all the other reports and information. (Fostering, single)

The interview data indicated that some practitioners who used the CPR for long-term/permanent foster placements liked the thoroughness of the report and felt it was necessary to complete, regardless of whether the child was to be placed in a long-term/permanent foster placement or adoption. The reasons offered, however, were not only about achieving accurate best interests and matching decisions, but about providing a helpful record for the child to return to in the future.

If I try and put myself in that child's shoes as they get older and they want to know what decisions were made and why, then I would think that a decision to separate me from my birth family permanently, should have the same scrutiny and the same sort of information, whether it's via long-term fostering or adoption. (Panel Chair, dual)

However, many practitioners who used the permanence report for long-term/permanent foster placements found that it was too geared towards adoption and was difficult to use.

We find it very unwieldy indeed . . . It is biased towards adoption. I think it is biased possibly towards meeting the legal requirements of these matters rather than being user friendly for both the author and the carer/reader. (LAC, single)

Many practitioners felt that long-term/permanent foster care was too often seen as not needing the same level of robust reporting as adoption, again evidencing the perception of long-term or permanent foster care as a "Cinderella service" (Lowe and Murch *et al*, 2002, p. 147). Here again, though, the emphasis was on whether information needed to be available for the future through the report being on file, rather than the extent to which the CPR would improve the quality of decision making.

It would depend on the level of the social worker's knowledge and skill and understanding in completing the CPR, but on the whole I think there is almost the assumption that if you are going to foster you don't need as much information as if you are going to adopt because there are always going to be social workers around. (Fostering, dual)

Those practitioners whose local authorities did not use a permanence report simply stated that they did not do so because it was designed for adoption not fostering and some used the old Form E along with the other paperwork instead:

We use the Form E, we don't use a CPR because that is obviously for adoption. We then have all the other kinds of supporting paperwork so if we are doing an advice for permanent fostering then we would expect to see that coming before panel, we would expect to see a Form

E, up-to-date school reports, their BAAF medicals and a foster carer's report and then for the match we would have all of those plus the Form F on the carers and a matching report. (Fostering, single)

One authority had designed their own report format. They felt that their report worked well and was as thorough but more appropriate to long-term/permanent foster care than the permanence report.

Panel were saying that the child's permanence report didn't provide them with the sort of information that they needed to make those decisions ... So they asked whether we could look at developing something so we developed our own, pulling information from the old Form E and adding it to parts of the child's permanence report and thinking about how we evidence the matching for the child. So it was an amalgamation. (Fostering, single)

As with other aspects of practice, where local authorities do take new steps in developing practice, it is important to build in a review over time, and this local authority was reviewing their reporting format in the light of experience.

The use of children's certificates in long-term and permanent foster care

Several authorities reported that they provided children who were being placed in long-term/permanent placements or were in an existing short-term placement changing to long-term/permanent with a certificate to mark the occasion and to confirm the placement as their permanent family. Those authorities who did this felt that it had been successful and the children had responded well.

We do give out a certificate – they get a certificate if they are going to be long-term. I did a review this morning and the carer – one of the children she cares for became long term linked with her in the last few months – and she said, 'His certificate is up on the wall' and when I went up to the bedroom there it was and he is clearly very proud of his certificate which says he is long term. (IRO, single)

When this was raised in interviews as a possibility, authorities which did not use certificates said they had not thought about it before but felt it might be a good idea in some circumstances. They felt that it would communicate that the placement was the child's permanent family, similar to adoption practice, with the aim of making the child feel more secure and providing stability within the placement.

> *It would be an overt statement of something that the child could relate to and I think it is quite an abstract concept to say you can stay with us permanently and depending on the child's level of understanding that may or may not have real meaning for them. But I think if you did use a certificate to say this formal process has been approved and we are all backing it, that would be quite a strong statement for the child to be able to recognise and refer back to and obviously something that they could put into their life history book as well.* (Fostering, dual)

Some of the practitioners commented that a certificate would not be suitable for every child, especially in the older age range. Some young people had strong ties to their birth family and there was a risk of rejection of the placement if they felt they had to choose or identify more with the foster family.

> *Certainly for those children who are in a permanent placement, where we are working with the intention of reducing the role of birth families, giving the child a certificate to stick on a bedroom wall – I mean it is a bit like rubbing salt in wounds, isn't it?* (Fostering, dual)

Several practitioners noted that, even though a foster placement is meant to be long-term/permanent, it cannot be guaranteed that it will last and the additional marker of commitment might make a subsequent loss feel all the greater.

> *I have seen too many breakdowns . . . I can see that some children would say, 'So much for that!' sort of thing, you know. 'You give me this and it has not worked out.'* (LAC, single)

The opposite might also be the case, where children may have been in their foster placement a while, see their foster family as a "normal" family and would find the certificates stigmatising.

There are some long-term stable placements where they almost don't want to recognise that they are being looked after. So I can see some children saying, 'Well, you know, this is my home. I don't want a certificate to say I have been at home for that time.' (LAC, single)

These varied comments on what is quite a specific piece of practice are excellent demonstrations of how any procedure or practice needs to be applied with very great care and with sensitivity to the nuanced meanings that placements and families, foster and birth, have for individual children and young people.

5 Social work practice with children in long-term or permanent placements

In the area of practice with children and young people, once the match was agreed and the child was in a planned placement, there were several elements that were covered in the questionnaires and followed up in interviews and focus groups. This process was to some extent selective, but included key areas for permanence ranging from team structures and practices, through life story work, parenting roles and decisions, LAC reviews and leaving care.

Specialist teams, workers and training

It was important when investigating the extent to which supporting long-term or permanent foster care had become a defined and specific social work activity to consider whether team structures reflected a move in this direction. Local authorities were asked whether they had child and family workers or teams who specialised in working with children in long-term or permanent placements and whether specialist training on permanence was provided.

Less than half of local authorities responded that they had specialist workers or teams for children in long-term/permanent placements, but most of these seemed to be looked after children teams who were specialist in the sense of planning for and supporting looked after children in a range of placements and *not* having competing work in child protection. While there were no significant differences between systems in having specialist teams, there was a trend for fewer authorities with the dual system to have separate teams compared to authorities with the single system (S 46%, 23; LTD 20%, 4; PD 29%, 6).

Most looked after children teams were responsible for children in what might loosely be called permanence plans, but this could be in a range of placements.

We have a looked after children team whose caseloads consist of a lot of children in permanent foster care, but they also deal with children/ young people who are in residential care or placed with parents. (Questionnaire, LAC, single)

Many of the practitioners with this arrangement stated that it worked well and that it allowed the full support of long-term/permanent placements to happen and for social workers to build up expertise and really know the children:

This structure has enabled greater focus to be placed upon "permanency" for children looked after. (Questionnaire LAC single).

In response to the question on training, 50 per cent (34) of local authorities were said to offer social workers post-qualifying training on long-term/permanent fostering and there were no differences between single and dual systems. Significantly more local authorities with specialist teams offered post-qualifying training on long-term/permanent foster care (79%, 21) compared to authorities without separate teams (33%, 13).[11] It was not clear what kind of training was included here, but authorities mentioned topics such as attachment and resilience, which are relevant for permanence but not exclusive to it.

Caseloads and visits

There has been some suggestion in other research that long-stay foster children may receive less frequent visits from children's social workers than short-term children (Beek and Schofield, 2004a). The questionnaire asked both about caseloads and frequency of visits to children.

Most responses about *caseloads* were qualified by the understandable comment that it was hard to give figures for certain types of cases on caseloads across teams. But the average estimated total of long-term/permanent fostering cases ranged from 1–20, with a mean of 6. The proportions ranged from seven per cent of total caseload to 100 per cent

---

[11] $\chi2 = 13.22$, $df = 1$, $p<0.01$

of total caseload (suggesting a high degree of specialisation for some individual workers) but with a mean of 39 per cent. There were no differences between single and dual systems.

The majority, 64 per cent (40), of local authorities stated that they *visited* children in long-term/permanent placements at least every three months, which is the statutory level and 36 per cent (22) at least monthly or every six weeks. There were no authorities which had a policy of visiting the children fortnightly and none who said that they visited less than every three months and there were no differences between single and dual systems. Here again, though, responses were qualified with the comment that frequency of visits depended on the child's needs at the time.

The interviews suggested that in some authorities the LAC teams tried to make sure that children in a long-term/permanent placement received the same level of support and visits from their social worker as children in other types of placements. However, there was a tendency in other authorities for the child's social worker to visit the placement less than other types of placement because these placements were usually stable and social workers had to prioritise children at risk.

I think they would hope it is long-term and would seek to support the foster family where they need it. But obviously, settled children receive less attention from a social worker than children that are at risk, immediately at risk, and that is one of the conundrums of the whole role of social work in child care. (LAC, single)

Some of the foster carers in the focus groups found that a change of status of placement had resulted in reduced visits from the child's social worker.

When my child was moved from short-term to long-term, even though it wasn't a physical move, you know, it was just a move in the type of placement, I was told by her social worker that her visits rather than being a six-weekly requirement became a six-monthly requirement . . . The justification behind that which I was given is that it is a settled placement. However, this child hadn't changed and every placement she has had was settled until it broke down – so how settled is settled? (Foster carer)

There were no significant differences between authorities which had separate teams and the frequency with which they visited children. However, those practitioners with separate LAC and child protection teams felt that at least children in long-term/permanent placements did not receive less support because social workers were diverted to child protection work.

We have a separate looked after children's team and they specialise in work with the children in the long-term placements. Whether they are actually matched or are children where all the proceedings are done with and they are either waiting for a permanent placement or in one, the LAC team looks after all of those. So they don't have to prioritise child protection. (Fostering, single)

Concern about staff turnover among social workers with responsibility for children in care generally, and in long-term/permanent placements in particular, was widespread across very different authorities. IFPs, which were providing placements, sometimes felt they had to fill in the gaps for the children. Local authority practitioners were only too aware of the problems for children who experienced several changes of social worker. This resulted in inconsistency and infrequent visits.

I think quite often children have lots of different social workers. I think consistency is so important . . . the same face, the same person that's rooting for them. Getting to know different social workers, telling your story over and over again is very difficult. (IRO, dual)

Foster carers commented that the children's new social workers often did not have the full information about their child and that reading the child's Form E was not as valuable for offering support as really getting to know the child. They also commented on the lack of visits.

[Child] hasn't seen a social worker since last year and yet decisions have been made for him on the basis that nobody knows him. When we were given [child] we had a 42-page information sheet on him that actually said nothing because when this child came into our care even I would have said this is not the child you had . . . Quite often they don't know the child. (Foster carer)

However, some of the foster carers had very positive experiences with their child's social worker and felt that they were very much available to support them and their foster children.

> *When [child] was short term, the social worker was the one who fought for him to stay with us and sorted out the finances because he knew [child] was in the right place. Whereas a lot of other social workers could have said, 'I'm out, it's too much hassle'.* (Foster carer)

What worked best of all was where there was regular support and visits which were co-ordinated between the child's social worker and the fostering social worker. One foster carer from an IFP spoke movingly in a focus group of how, with a very difficult child in her first placement, the IFP supervising social worker and the local authority social worker for the child communicated so well with each other and with her that she felt as if they provided a 'cushion' of support for her.

Life story work

Life story work is seen in adoption practice as an essential part of both recording and helping the child to come to terms with the past as well as developing a coherent narrative to take towards the future (Ryan and Walker, 2007). It was therefore an important part of this study to see whether there were thought to be the same needs for a child with a permanence plan in foster care and the same commitment of time and expertise to the work.

Life story work in long-term/permanent foster care was said to be routine in 63 per cent (42) of local authorities. This modest figure may indicate differences in how authorities approached and thought about long-term/permanent foster placements in terms of the child's needs, in particular, distinguishing them from adoption. But alternatively, or additionally, it may show variation in the skills or resources made available by the local authorities for this work with foster children.

There was a significant difference between single and dual systems in the provision of life story work.[12] There was a trend for fewer dual system

---

[12] $\chi 2 = 6.64$, $df = 1$, $p<0.05$

local authorities to undertake life story work in long-term foster care cases compared to single system authorities and permanent foster care in the dual system (S 68%, 32; LTD 35%, 7; PD 50%, 9). There was no significant association between whether life story work was provided and whether the authority had a specialist LAC team, which is perhaps surprising.

Nearly all study local authorities which did not carry out life story work routinely in long-term/permanent placement stated that this was because of work pressures and ideally they would want to do more. They made comparisons with adoption, where life story work was a matter of course and suggested that this work in adoption often took priority over the needs of foster children – even though foster children's needs were acknowledged.

> *Life story work is not always offered as routine and often not offered. With adoption it is always offered. The child's social worker or family support worker may do direct work or sometimes it is contracted out to specialist independent workers. This is an area that does need tightening up on, as I understand some recent research shows many young people who have been in permanent foster care have very little understanding or information on family history or why they came into care and find it difficult to get this information in later life. The importance placed on this work for adoptees should also be applied to children who are placed permanently. Children who stay on in existing placements are the most likely not to have this work identified, especially those placed long term.* (Questionnaire, fostering, dual)

This account suggests that permanent plans are no guarantee of life story work, but that long-term plans in dual system authorities may reduce still further the likelihood of receiving life story work. It seems possible that such differentiations – between adoption and foster care, between permanent and long-term and between older and younger children – may be driven by resource constraints, but are also based on the idea that life story work is really only needed when children (often younger children) move into new and probably adoptive families. Whereas, in fact, even teenagers in long-term/permanent foster care with frequent contact with birth families may not have a coherent picture of their lives. They need the full range of what sensitive life story work has to offer, including the most basic record of information but also a chance to make sense of their complex past before setting off into adult life.

The questionnaire and interview responses indicated that life story work was undertaken by a range of practitioners. These included the child's social worker, the fostering social worker, the foster carers and commissioned independent workers. Two local authorities said that they had a specialist life story worker whose job it was to make sure that children in long-term/permanent placements, as well as adoptive placements, had life story work.

We have a dedicated life story worker, a qualified worker within the team with the LAC service. She doesn't do all the life story work – she does it on prioritised cases, but she also advises the rest of the staff on how to deal with life story work. It is a key focus of all of our permanence work. (LAC, single)

However, both local authorities commented that the service was in high demand and there could be a waiting list.

A referral to the life story worker is made and the wait is very, very long. (Questionnaire IRO, single)

Where it is difficult to ensure that busy workers have or find time for life story work, it does seem to be an advantage to have a worker who has expertise, but also who can keep the work on the team's agenda and support colleagues. On the other hand, if life story work became routine in long-term and permanent foster care, as it is in adoption, supervision by team leaders would automatically discuss it and fostering and other panels which recommend matches would look for evidence in the documentation that life story work had been done. Then it could become standard practice rather than something which was optional.

Independent fostering providers and work with the child

Although IFPs are fostering agencies that provide placements, it seems likely that their role in planning and supporting placements might include work with the child. This may be even more likely where placements are at a distance from the home authority. With the growth of the independent sector, this is no longer as common at it once was, but where geographical distance does occur, it is still a challenge for local authority and IFP social workers in terms of supporting children and managing placements.

Involvement in assessment, preparation and support of children varied between study IFPs. Around two-thirds reported being involved in assessing needs and preparing the child, and almost three-quarters in contributing to the child's permanence report (Table 5.2).

Table 5.2
IFP involvement in assessment and preparation of the child

	Single (n=21)	Long-term dual (n=46)	Permanent dual (n=45)
Assessment of child's needs	52%	65%	64%
Contributing to the permanence report	71%	67%	73%
Preparing the child for permanence e.g. life story work	48%	63%	60%

IFPs also described being involved in the assessment, preparation and support of the child by arranging or providing therapy, introductory visits, informal supervision, formal meetings with the child, helping carers to prepare the child, and getting advice from educational consultants and input to schools. Although some of this work may have been by default i.e. in the absence of an active or available child's social worker, specific pieces of work (such as life story work) were commissioned. As in local authorities, it is inevitable that supervision of foster carers will focus on the parenting task in relation to the child, and so IFP supervising social workers become knowledgeable about and, to some extent, inevitably active on behalf of the child.

Parenting roles and decision making

We have come to know over the years from diverse research (Sinclair, 2005; Schofield, 2003) and policy initiatives such as *Care Matters* (DCSF, 2007a) that what children say they want from their long-term foster families is the feeling of being normal and ordinary – not singled out and different. Part of that experience of normal life in families relates to the ways in which parenting roles are exercised and parenting decisions are made. Children look to their parents to love, protect and guide them. Foster carers in long-term and permanent placements are acting as parents and need to be able to fulfil that role convincingly for the children in their care.

There are no legal differences between the rights and responsibilities of birth, corporate and foster parents in short-term or in long-term/ permanent foster care. Nevertheless, as the range of definitions and care planning systems makes clear, attempts are being made at the level of local policy and procedure to carve out meanings and expectations of foster family life – in order to indicate that, regardless of the lack of legal differentiation, these are special and specific kinds of families for children when foster care is a permanent plan.

From the survey, interview and focus group data, there appear to be some general principles in each local authority in terms of how foster parents, birth parents and social workers might be viewed as parent figures in different placements. But there was considerable variation even within local authorities in the extent to which, for example, permanent foster carers were able to make certain kinds of decisions about school trips. Even if there were to be some overall statement of principle on such issues, the detail for each child, foster family and birth family would need to be settled at the level of the *placement agreement*.

Most authorities in the study make the initial decision over parenting roles and decision making at a placement agreement meeting at the start of the placement and may revise these if it changes to a long-term/ permanent placement. This process of creating a placement agreement happens outside of the rest of the care planning and placement review system, even though it must implement decisions, about contact for example, that are made elsewhere. Decisions made in a placement agreement meeting will also effectively be reviewed at the LAC review, since as a review of the placement plan it will have to deal with issues that have arisen as a result of the terms of the placement agreement. As this IRO comments, this is another area where parallel and interlinking planning processes are not always clearly co-ordinated.

> *The fostering social worker, the foster carer, the social worker and the parents, if they are around, sit down and they have a placement meeting where all these day-to-day arrangements are agreed. So that's outside of the LAC review which I'm involved in. But it's an important meeting really. It sets the scene for the foster carer . . . and they set the child's routines the same as they were at home, if they are appropriate of course. They talk about medication and what tablets they're on, bedtimes and all that kind of thing and that takes place in the placement planning meeting.* (IRO, dual)

> *The placement agreement is set out at placement agreement meetings and then confirmed at LAC reviews.* (Fostering, single)

Given the potential importance of the placement agreement, it was interesting that there were so few references to it in the data from the questionnaires, interviews or focus groups. Perhaps it is seen as relevant in transitions from birth family to foster family – as implied by the IRO above – but less significant further down the road. However, although not formally part of the care planning process, the relative role of birth parents, foster carers, child and fostering social workers at the placement agreement meeting – and the availability or otherwise of reports used for the child's match with the carer, for example – would be significant in setting the tone for the placement and putting into effect the intentions of the long-term or permanent plan that had been decided at the relevant panel or in court.

In investigating the issue of *parental decision making* in greater detail in the survey, questions were asked about a range of very specific decisions. These were diet, clothes, haircuts, school, attendance at parents' evenings, school trips, overnight stays, foster family trips abroad and contact. It seemed likely, and was confirmed at the questionnaire piloting stage, that it was rarely the case that any decision was made by one person without consultation – so the questions were phrased in terms of which person or people would take the "lead roles" in making certain decisions, anticipating that for most decisions this lead role would still be shared by different combinations of people. We stated in the question the assumption that children would be consulted on all decisions, though of course there would be situations where they too may become lead decision makers.

We also selected two variables to test that seemed likely to affect parental decision making. The first was children's legal status (s31 or s20), since whether local authorities had legal parental responsibility or not seemed likely to make a difference to their perceived role and the role of birth parents and carers. Within these two different legal statuses, the second variable (as elsewhere in the project) was potential differences between authorities who had single or dual systems – and, within the dual systems, whether there were differences between long-term and permanent placements.

A number of questionnaire respondents still pointed out that it was difficult to answer these questions, as who took the lead or even influenced decisions depended so much on individual circumstances. Nevertheless, the responses did at least give some sense of the perceived balance of parenting power and responsibility in practice within different legal statuses and care plans and on very different decisions affecting the foster child.

Before looking at the results in detail, it is worth saying that there were very few statistically significant associations between who took the lead in decision-making and either the single/dual systems of care planning or the separate long-term and permanent routes within dual systems. This was something of a surprise given the emphasis in dual systems on the difference between long-term and permanent placements. But perhaps, overall, the similarities between long-term and permanent placements are more striking than the differences because of the shared legal context.

The constraints of the children's care status (whether under s31 or s20) make it inevitable that decisions are shared. For the child to feel ordinary and in a normal family, the potentially complex and time-consuming process of seeking or negotiating permissions needs to be efficient, transparent and almost certainly more empowering of foster carers than at present. This would certainly be the verdict of the foster carer focus groups in this study. Carers understood the need for some degree of external scrutiny, but had drastic stories to tell of cancelled family holidays, when a passport for the new foster child had not been obtained in time, or children nearly missing something as simple as the school class walk to the local library, just because the form needed a senior social worker's signature that was delayed. Some carers suggested that, for example, all children in long-term foster care should have a passport obtained for them at the point of the plan, so that the family would be able to take trips more easily. Children's lives are expected to be enriched by their experience of foster family life – but there appears to be a risk that delays and restrictions can jeopardise these opportunities.

Making parenting decisions about children on care orders (CA 1989 s31)

Out of the mass of data from the parenting questions for children on care orders, we identified some relevant findings for each potential decision maker.

Foster carers

The majority of local authorities and IFPs stated that foster carers had a lead role in day-to-day decisions, such as diet, clothes and haircuts (see Table 5.3 below). Over three-quarters of local authorities and IFPs also said that foster carers took a lead in making decisions about overnight stays. It was interesting that out of the more significant decisions that could be made, overnight stays were singled out as appropriate for foster carers; interesting but not surprising, as this was an area targeted by more permissive government guidance which arose in response to the overwhelming concern of children and young people that the problem of simply staying overnight with a friend, including the friend's parents having to have a criminal records check, was one of the most negative aspects of being in foster care. The lesson here may be that national guidance of this kind can take the burden of risk-taking away from local authorities and improve the lives of foster children and foster families, especially those in longer term placements.

Over half of both IFPs and local authorities said that carers could make decisions about school trips. Around two-thirds of IFPs stated that carers had a say in the school the child attends. However, with local authorities there appeared to be differences between systems on this issue, with 70 per cent (41) of single system local authorities stating that foster carers had a lead role compared to 44 per cent (12) in the long-term/dual system and 41 per cent (11) in the permanent /dual system.[13]

One perhaps surprising result was that less than one in five local authorities and IFPs stated that foster carers played a lead role in *decisions about contact* with the birth family. This might be understandable where children were in short-term care and contact decisions were being made in the context of a plan to return home. However, it seems that where a child is entrusted to a foster family to bring up to adult life, the carers should be closely involved in decisions about how the relationship with the birth family through contact is managed, and indeed facilitated, in the best interests of the child. Research has certainly found that, for carers, a lack of consultation about difficult contact for children can put the long-term placement at risk (Beek and Schofield, 2004b).

One of the challenges for IFPs regarding decision-making powers delegated to their foster carers was related to the range of systems, placements and perspectives in the local authorities for whom they provide placements. Although placement agreements should settle the parenting decision-making roles, for most children there will always be decisions emerging that may not have been anticipated. It was reported that the IFP foster carer and the IFP social worker cannot assume anything, because each child's social worker will handle the situation differently. So unless placement agreements are very clearly worded, IFP carers may have difficulty in keeping within the expectations of the care authority.

---

[13] $\chi2 = 8.38$, $df = 1$, $p<0.05$

The child's social worker

The role of the child's social worker as decision maker is almost as contentious as that of the foster carer (Beek and Schofield, 2004a), for different and yet related reasons. Social workers are not trying to be "ordinary" parents, but they do feel responsible at a personal as well as professional level for the child's welfare and happiness, responding to the needs and requests of the child (and the foster carer and birth parent) while also having to ensure that they are carrying out the letter and intentions of any plan agreed in court and at planning meetings. As with other areas of social work decision making, social workers balance their autonomy with both organisational constraints and supports.

In the survey there were no significant differences between single and dual systems in relation to the perceived role of the social worker as decision makers for long-term/permanent fostered children on care orders. Just under 10 per cent of local authorities said that the child's social worker would take a lead role in deciding diet, clothes, and haircuts. About twice as many IFPs stated that social workers took a lead role in these decisions. Around three-quarters of local authorities and IFPs stated that the child's social worker takes a lead role in deciding on the school the child attends and around a third of local authorities and IFPs stated that the social worker had a lead role in choosing who attends parents' evenings. Around three-quarters of local authorities and IFPs stated that the children's social worker had a lead role in permission for school trips and around half of local authorities and IFPs stated that they had a lead role in making decisions about staying overnight with friends. This suggests that, although foster carers are able to take responsibility for this decision in some cases and to some degree, social workers would still be involved in many situations. Almost all local authorities and IFPs stated that social workers had a lead role in deciding on trips abroad and contact arrangements with the birth family.

More likely to be involved in the big decisions, for example about choice of school, social workers nevertheless can get caught up in complicated dynamics at the interface between foster and birth families and between the families and the social work and other professional agencies over even relatively minor decisions. Social workers admitted it was not always clear how decision making should be managed. They acknowledged the arguments for greater autonomy for foster carers in placements planned to be permanent, while experiencing a sense of responsibility on their own behalf and on behalf of the organisation for the child's welfare. It seemed likely that different social workers managed this balance differently in relation to delegating powers on a day-to-day basis or keeping a closer grip, and that the availability of support from their organisation would affect the level of risk they felt they could live with. IFPs reported how, although these inter-agency and intra-agency differences of approach were understandable, they could make it difficult sometimes for foster carers who related to different social workers from different local authorities – and foster carers within local authorities reported experiencing something rather similar in terms of individual differences between social workers even from the same team.

Negotiation about decisions for each child in placement agreements and at LAC reviews, as well as between meetings, is an ongoing but important process that needs to be handled well. Some risks may need to be taken in the context of trust in the foster carer. One foster carer in a focus group, who also happened to be a social worker for a neighbouring authority, commented on how frustrating it could be for both sides. As a foster carer he wanted quicker decisions than was often possible – and as a social worker he and his colleagues found that they were often being chased through meetings and into court by messages from foster carers needing urgent decisions on relatively minor matters. In both roles he was aware of the impact of delay on the children and the foster families – and wished for clearer guidance that might help social workers to make the right judgements about which foster carers could be allowed to make which decisions. Knowing whether this is a personal risk as a social worker or foster carer or an organisationally sanctioned risk would be helpful.

Birth parents
The role of birth parents in cases where children are placed on care orders in permanent/long-term foster care, and where their right to exercise parental responsibility is dictated by the local authority, will vary inevitably and appropriately from case to case. Nevertheless, the social

work principles of working in partnership with parents, valuing their role in children's lives and facilitating reasonable contact suggests that important negotiations over decision making have to be conducted here too.

A minority of local authorities and IFPs stated that birth parents took the lead on any of the decisions and there were no significant differences between systems. Just over a quarter of local authorities stated that birth parents took a lead role in decisions about haircuts, school choice, parents' evenings, school trips, and trips abroad. Under one in five local authorities stated that they took a lead role in diet, clothes, overnight stays, and contact. IFPs saw a similar pattern, with only around a quarter suggesting that birth parents took the lead role in any of the decisions.

What was often stressed in the more open comment boxes on questionnaires was that although parents may not be playing a lead role in taking decisions, it was good practice to consult parents on all decisions. For the IFPs, much of the work with birth parents over decisions would be expected to be done by the local authority child's social worker. But because contact arrangements affected the child and the foster family, there was sometimes a need for speedy discussions with birth parents. IFP workers and carers would take on this role at certain times where appropriate.

Independent reviewing officer

The independent reviewing officer (IRO) is a role developed initially to answer concerns of the courts (who had been given a clear message that they could not keep control of cases after plans had been agreed and court orders made) to ensure that plans were followed by local authorities. Courts could rely, they were told, on the new IROs to use their role in chairing LAC reviews to monitor the implementation of plans. IROs were also given the duty to make a referral to CAFCASS's legal section to take the case back to court if they felt that the local authority had not taken all appropriate steps to implement a court sanctioned care plan.

The IRO role was still evolving at the time that the agency survey for this study was undertaken at the beginning of 2007. But in principle the IRO has the potential to play an important monitoring role and, because of their overview of cases, to help local authorities to improve their planning and practice. In our interviews with IROs, they had a strong sense of the potential importance of their role, but raised some concerns about how independent they were perceived to be and also about the fact that they were limited to chairing LAC reviews that were only able to make recommendations rather than decisions. (See section below on LAC reviews.)

Even though IROs are not expected to be making parenting decisions as such we included them in the questions on decision making in case practice was perceived to be rather different on the ground. In fact, across the range of decisions in the survey, from hair cuts to choice of school and trips abroad, fewer than 10 per cent of local authorities and IFPs saw IROs as taking a lead role in decision making. The only area of decision making that IROs were seen as rather more influential in was contact – but even here less than 20 per cent of local authorities and just under a third of IFPs saw IROs as taking a lead role in contact decisions

Making parenting decisions about accommodated children (CA 1989 s20)

As discussed in the legal and care planning sections above, the fact that children could be subject to either long-term or permanent foster care plans while the birth parents held sole parental responsibility could be seen as offering the potential for collaboration or for difficult battles for control or periods of both across a placement. Such outcomes might depend on a range of circumstances and the attitude of both the parents with parental responsibility and the local authority, with decision making about day-to-day as well as major decisions being an important issue.

There were few differences (Table 5.3) between single and dual systems when it came to expectations of who would be more likely to take the lead on different decisions. Interestingly, the only differences were that in single system local authorities, carers took more of a lead in decision making than long-term and permanent carers in dual system authorities.

There were some useful comparisons between decision making in the different systems for children on care orders and accommodated children

Table 5.3
Foster carer takes lead role in different systems/ legal status

System	Single		Long-term dual		Permanent dual	
Legal status	CO (n = 59)	S20 (n = 51)	CO (n = 27)	S20 (n = 25)	CO (n = 27)	S20 (n = 23)
Child's diet	100%	92%	100%	84%	96%	83%
Child's clothes	100%	96%	96%	76%	100%	79%
Haircuts	93%	77%	85%	48%	89%	52%
Which school the child attends	70%	57%	44%	20%	41%	26%
Who attends parents' evenings	88%	80%	70%	36%	74%	39%
Permission for school trips	51%	49%	52%	16%	48%	17%
Staying overnight with friends	85%	71%	78%	36%	78%	39%
Foster family trips abroad	51%	61%	37%	16%	41%	17%
Contact with birth family	17%	29%	19%	8%	19%	9%

but, in general terms, the message was that, although birth parents were the sole holders of parental responsibility under s20, they were not perceived as "controlling" placements for accommodated children.

Do long-term/permanent foster carers in practice make more parenting decisions than task-centred carers?

Important in this area is whether decision making rights and responsibilities change once children become subject of long-term or permanent plans – issues that were common to children on care orders and accommodated. The interview data and focus groups suggested that key parenting roles, which are more likely to be delegated to long-term/ permanent carers, included deciding on overnight stays at friends' houses, in line with recent guidance (as mentioned above), permission for school trips, and the management of contact.

Permanent carers should be able to agree a sleepover for their child or should be able to agree school trips, you know, so that they can just get on and do the trip to a local farm park. I think things like managing the contact arrangements, but not changing the contact arrangements. (Fostering, dual)

However, some practitioners stated that the decisions about school trips still lay with them and they would need to give permission rather than be informed.

If you want to go on a school trip we have to sign, you know, the social worker has to sign consent for that. Carers can't give consent to those kinds of things because the local authority has the legal responsibility for the child. (LAC, dual)

As elsewhere, there was variation in the way different authorities, and perhaps teams, approached parenting roles and the extent to which – as in this comment – a legal interpretation determined them. Many practitioners commented that they felt bound by the fact that legally there was no difference between a short-term placement and a long-term/permanent placement when it came to decisions about the children.

Legally, carers can't have a different level of responsibility – what they can have is delegated and . . . delegated responsibilities are still based on the child, the family and all of those people having a say in the decision. (Fostering, dual)

In the interviews, most practitioners confirmed that carers were not allowed lead responsibility on decisions about holidays abroad, which school the child attended, or about medical procedures. But even on minor issues such as hair cuts, birth parents need time to come to terms with the loss of role and, hopefully, to trust the carers.

Even with a care order the parents retain PR. The extent to which we can delegate PR to a foster carer is limited on a day-to-day basis. Obviously, the longer the child is in placement, the more you expect the carers to exercise day-to-day responsibility I suppose. But no, I think the major decisions in life – which school does this child go to, does he have to go and have his medicals, you know those sorts of things don't change very much. It will be more the 'How often am I going to have the kid's hair cut?', 'What style am I going to let him have?', you know that will be left to the carer. You know increasing as the placement progresses, because parents would expect that as well. Parents can get very unhappy about foster carers exercising even that sort of decision making for children who have gone straight into a placement, because it does represent a real loss of responsibility for their children. (Fostering, dual)

The fact that decision-making roles change "as the placement progresses" implies that it may be better to negotiate gradual changes so that foster carers have earned the trust of children and birth parents – and social workers – to be able to make more and more significant decisions about the child. Whether these discussions and negotiations are best held at LAC reviews, or away from the formality and presence of external people, will depend very much on each case. But it is likely that both foster carers and birth parents – and children – would find it easier to be part of a gentle round of negotiations later ratified by meeting, if necessary, rather than given a single meeting to speak up, debate and reach conclusions.

As the questionnaire data suggested, practitioners explained how, overall, most long-term/permanent carers made more of the day-to-day decisions about the child than short-term carers. They felt that this was necessary in order for the placement to run smoothly and was also simply common sense. If a child had been in placement for a number of years, there was no need for the social worker to be contacted for most things.

Even for something as basic, say, like a haircut, if it was a short-term placement, I think you would probably talk to the social worker who would talk to the parents because the parents may have a certain place they take them to or they may want it done in a certain way. But in a long-term placement, I think as a carer you are much more likely to take that sort of decision yourself really; you would just go ahead and do it as part of the normal family routine. (IRO, dual)

Foster carers agreed with this, if only because of the time it took to get permissions.

When I did the training it was, like, well, there has got to be an amount of common sense here because if they have a school trip coming up, by the time you have got the forms to the social worker, the social worker sends it to mum and mum has got it back to the social worker, the social worker has got back to you, they have been back six months! You know, at the end of the day we have to use common sense. (Foster carer)

Having good relationships between long-term/permanent carers and birth parents was thought to be essential by both practitioners and foster carers for making delegated parenting roles work.

Foster carers can very much see the role of birth parents and link with them, it can work very well. (LAC, single)

However, a few of the foster carers spoke of how hard it was to maintain this collaborative relationship when it came to consulting with birth parents who had significant difficulties.

My boy [child] is my latest, and he has a special needs mum so she wouldn't have any understanding as to what she would be agreeing to. And my other two boys' mum is alcoholic and you can never find her. (Foster carer)

Some practitioners commented that foster carers liked the fact that they had to consult the parents and local authority about decisions because of the legal status of the placement. This liking for shared responsibility was reflected in some of the foster carers' comments too.

I think I am happy at the level that he is at because I would always want to have support with decisions. I wouldn't want to become complacent and end up doing something that I may not have approval for. We don't have difficulty contacting somebody who can give that advice, whether it is your own supervising social worker, the manager of the team or somebody who is on duty for the team. Somebody is available all the time when you are in doubt. (Foster carer)

This carer was in a large single system local authority, which had a specialist support team for long-term carers, with a team leader who was known to the carers as a respected advocate for them. This availability of workers who would know them and their children and could be trusted is a reminder of the way in which being given and accepting delegated parental responsibility for often troubled and challenging children works better if carers also feel they have a secure base in the support team.

Looked after children (LAC) reviews

In turning to a consideration of the role of the statutory LAC review in planning and supporting long-term/permanent placements, the situation for local authorities and IFPs revolved around two core, related but rather different, issues. The first was the role of the LAC review in permanency planning and ensuring that plans were implemented in the short, medium and longer term. The second was the perception of children's and carers' experiences of attending reviews in long-term and permanent placements. Indirectly linked to this, was the question of whether reviews in these placements were helpful and necessary or intrusive and problematic – or perhaps both. Both these issues raise important questions about the various roles of the LAC review in the context of long-term/permanent placements.

With regard to the place of LAC reviews in planning and reviewing plans, it was made clear by our respondents, especially the independent reviewing officers (IROs), that LAC reviews are not designed to generate plans but only to review them. Of course, as discussed above, if a review effectively proposes steps to expedite a plan or proposes making changes to a plan as a result of the review process then the LAC review is still key to care planning and implementation – even if other meetings or individual managers go on to make "decisions".

As LAC review Chairs, IROs are key to this process. In this study there were comments about the timing of their first significant involvement in permanency planning and what this meant for later reviews. In some local authorities, IROs were seen and saw themselves as involved from the point that children first came into care, as they would be notified of the need for timetabling early reviews. They would then be involved in the permanency planning process which occurs at the second review, though this is often building on a previous planning meeting that does not include the IRO. The reviewing task will be not only to ensure implementation in the short–term as placements are made, but also to consider the progress of placements in the longer term. It is both the initial input and the evolution of the LAC reviews over long placements that need some thought.

As so many local authorities and IFPs report that the majority of children who become subject of long-term and permanence plans are already in placements that may become long term, the plan is likely to have evolved over a period of reviews in any case. All the practitioners were in agreement that LAC reviews and IROs had a role to play in preventing children drifting in placements without a permanence plan – and so helping to ensure children had an appropriate long-term/permanent foster placement where this was the plan.

> *A good IRO will make sure that the plan is clear in terms of permanent fostering . . . like I had last week, not a notice of concern but an IRO raising an issue that we have as yet failed to identify a permanent placement for a child who is in temporary foster care. So I think it is those sorts of things – I do think they have a role.* (Fostering, dual)

> *We do the reviews. We will look at children who are in placement and one thing we do ask is, what are the plans for them? If the plans look like they are either drifting or they are going to be long-term then obviously we talk about whether the carers would be prepared to do it and then, if it is flagging, we tend to pass it back to the long-term linking people.* (IRO, single)

However, once a placement was matched as long-term/permanent, some practitioners and foster carers commented that the reviews (and the IROs) were not specific enough about or sensitive enough to long-term/permanency issues. One practitioner even went so far as to say that there should be different IROs for long-term/permanent and short-term cases.

> *I just think there is a need for a structure in permanency and the more structured it is the better. Obviously, we are structured in terms of planning around children that are in legal processes, but children that are not in legal processes, I am not sure that the planning is as robust as it might be. Independent reviewing officers may not have the*

expertise in permanency that is necessary in order to make appropriate plans . . . They obviously do the reviews, statutory reviews and they do a good job. But I don't know how much specific training they get any more than we as social workers get. So sometimes you can end up with plans to increase contact when the social work team is saying that that doesn't seem to be a good idea or decrease contact where it might be OK . . . I suppose it is around training and around IROs having their own specialist service where they have that body of knowledge. So maybe dividing independent reviewing officers into short-term and long-term would be a good idea so that they develop their own expertise and can be a source of advice and consultation as well. (LAC single)

Although it would probably not be realistic to have specialist IROs, it was clear that additional training around permanence was necessary. One concern was whether the questions asked at reviews were appropriately tailored to long-term/permanent placements. Many practitioners and foster carers mentioned the fact that, in the LAC review, the suitability of the placement and the care plan was brought up, as if for the first time, even if the placement had been running smoothly for a number of years. The question was also still asked about why the child could not return home, as foster carers in the focus groups confirmed. This is a difficult question for children and carers to hear each time, but is probably not welcome to birth parents either, if it means repeating every six months the reasons why the child was deemed at risk of significant harm.

R: Does the review still ask the question 'Why can't this child go home?' for example?

Yes they do. (Unanimous 'yes' from the foster carer group.)

R: Even in a planned long-term family?

We are a very settled family and I think the reviews are more of a hindrance. The children come through our door, and as I say the title "looked after" is put on their heads and that is how they feel. Because for six months they are like totally settled and then that comes through and it upsets the whole thing. The whole system upsets them.

The question of whether reviews are too intrusive is a difficult one. On the one hand, reviews are seen by policy makers as an essential part of the exercise of corporate responsibility for looked after children. On the other hand, the same policy makers who created the system see it as so intrusive for children that it becomes one argument for promoting special guardianship – a parenting status which invites no subsequent scrutiny of parenting or child welfare.

One element seen as important in terms of whether the LAC review was intrusive or not was whether review meetings were acceptable to children and whether they felt able to choose or wanted to attend. The foster carers said that children were always invited to attend. But the foster carers had a range of opinions about whether the children in their care liked attending their LAC reviews. Some suggested that the children were not really able to understand what it was about;

> *We try and explain to [child]. We have to put down a minimum of four sentences and it will be '[Social worker] and a friend are coming here', then you move on to say, 'They are coming to see if you are happy here', and then you move on.* (Foster carer)

Two foster carers stated that the children in their care enjoyed the review and found the preparatory activities fun.

> *For the first review he did the booklet and it was brilliant, he answered everything. But the second one I said would he like to go and he was delighted. He sat there through the whole review and he done fantastic, spoke out, everything.* (Foster carer)

However, some foster carers said that their children did not like attending their LAC review and had chosen not to because they did not like the formality of it when they saw themselves as in a normal family:

> *He don't like the fact that he has to fill a form in because he is saying, 'Well, you are saying you are a long-term mum and that is what they say you are, a long-term mum. You are our mum and then they come here and they will say . . .' And we basically have different forms: 'Do they look after you well?' So we don't feel important. And when they have the LAC review form especially, the oldest child will say, 'I really,*

really hate it'. I mean, most of the time he either rips them up or just puts 'Boring!' on them because he feels it is not important. (Foster carer)

The right of the child to participate in the review extends to completing a form which evaluates their foster carers – a request which makes sense in terms of the child's right to say what they think of their "placement". But as this carer above points out, it must seem strange to write six-monthly reports on your "long-term mum".

In one focus group, contrasting stories were offered of the approach taken by IROs to the child's attendance at reviews. The general picture was of children's expected attendance and therefore their feelings being given priority. But one foster carer described how her foster son had overcome his nervousness and started to attend and enjoy his review. His birth mother, who had not previously attended, decided that she would start to attend. When the foster child said he would be too anxious to go if his mother attended, the message from the IRO was said by the carer to be that the birth mother had a right to be there and the child must "toughen up".

IROs themselves said that they valued the child's attendance at reviews so that they could talk with the child – again an obvious piece of useful practice in some respects. But is the IRO's meeting with the child supposed to supplement/be an extra layer of scrutiny beyond the meetings that the child's social worker will have had with the child? Is a child allowed to choose not to attend a review without feeling under some pressure to do so because the IRO needs to see him or her? This is just one of the various areas where the IRO role may need to be clarified. Are they more like Chairs of meetings or independent social workers with direct relationships with children?

There were various other concerns voiced by foster carers about LAC reviews in longer-term placements. One foster carer described how, in her authority, it was policy that in order for the child or young person to feel comfortable to attend, no reference would be made to any negative behaviour.

At my young person's review she is always there and I have always encouraged her to be there. But as she has gone into adolescence, I mean she was EBD (emotional and behavioural difficulties) anyway, and now she has gone into adolescence there has been an increase in, you know, challenging behaviour, shall we say. But we can't address things in the review because she is there. Because it is the child's review you are not allowed to say anything negative. But in actual fact this is where they make the plan for the next six months. I have been picked up on it, the school has been picked up on it. . . (Foster carer)

This foster carer, and it seems the school, had been criticised for raising the child's negative behaviours at the LAC review. Although the principle behind this approach was understandable to a degree and problems could be raised outside the meeting, it seems likely that the young person would think it strange that a group of people meet and conclude that there were no problems that needed addressing, when presumably outside of the review concerns may be frequently raised with the young person herself.

The limited powers of the review were remarked on by IROs themselves: 'We cannot make decisions over anything; it's all recommendations' (IRO, dual). But foster carers commented that sometimes "recommendations" were put forward, but did not get followed up or acted upon between reviews. Carers had concerns that the IROs did not take strong enough steps to ensure recommendations were put into effect – and sometimes had tougher expectations of foster carers than social workers and schools.

My experience has been that although they have this "action section" in the review, don't they, you know things to be actioned after the review and who they are supposed to be actioned by – but actually you as a carer are the only person who gets a rap on the knuckles if you haven't done your stuff. There is stuff that has been on my young person's LAC review that has appeared every six months since, you know, creation and it never ever gets followed up and the Reviewing Officer will sit there and say, 'Have you done this?' and the social worker will say 'No, I haven't got round to that yet', and then move on and the school, 'Have you done this?' 'Um well we started to do it but we felt it was more important to do . . .', so 'OK' and then we move on.

So it appears for the next six months, because there isn't any price to pay as far as I can see. (Foster carer)

There were other examples of this uncertainty, part of which was about what the reviews were for. Some of the foster carers commented that the LAC review was being used for too many other purposes, even counting as a contact meeting for the child and birth parent.

The social worker has actually said if she [the child] did attend a review and it is at a venue, not at home, it would be classed as a contact anyway. (Foster carer)

Among the various roles that LAC reviews played, one foster carer mentioned that the LAC review doubled up as a time when the birth mother could see her social worker,

The social worker doesn't need to go and see the birth parent at home because they will be at the review. (Foster carer)

There is no doubt that the LAC review is a significant event for most children and foster carers and at times this may be overlooked by social workers in cases of stable long-term placements. One foster carer had an example when the proper LAC review did not take place and only amounted to a quick phone call.

At my last review, my 16-year-old, because she was 16, I kept saying to her, 'Your next review is really important, you have got to say what you want, what your long-term plans are, you know, there are going to be a lot of people there'. On the day of the review, there was actually a telephone call from somebody at admin saying the Reviewing Officer can't come out to see you today, are there any problems and that was it! (Foster carer)

In summary, the role of the LAC review in helping to ensure that care plans for permanency are made and avoiding drift in existing long-term cases is generally seen as necessary. But the *management* of LAC reviews as an ongoing part of the child's life in long-term care remains a challenge for everyone. In particular:
- A balance needs to be achieved. Some children and foster families will

find the process and the review meeting itself intrusive and want its role minimised. Others find it helpful and want to be sure it is given appropriate importance.

- The LAC review meeting can appear to take on too many roles and become a substitute in busy practitioners' lives for other kinds of more appropriate social work activity, especially around work with the birth parents but also meetings with medical professionals and school staff.
- Children and young people have rights to participate in whatever way they choose. This must extend to support for children whether they choose to attend reviews or not.

Although it might not be appropriate to have IROs who deal only with long-term/permanent cases, it must be desirable for there to be a collective attempt to ensure that each review is appropriate for the placement and the child. There is mention in the White Paper, *Care Matters – Time for Change* (Department for Education and Skills, 2007a, p. 132), that the role of IROs will be reinforced. Since the IRO role was largely to ensure that the care plan is made and implemented, some thinking needs to go on into how the role works when the review is about monitoring and supporting the ongoing nature of a placement through to adult life, rather than being a focus for planning and intervention. Although the IRO role in its origins was closely linked to the courts, a rather rigid, procedural or legalistic approach to reviewing placements may make it less effective in promoting a child's feeling of being part of the foster family as well as maintaining comfortable birth family links.

Leaving care

Apart from the child's general developmental and educational progress in placement, if there is one single issue that seems to define the success of a long-term or permanent foster placement, it is the leaving or not leaving of it. As discussed under definitions of care plans, both the placement pathways and the nature of the expected family commitment hinge on whether the placement will last till adulthood and then, in many cases, whether it is hoped and planned that it will last beyond the age of 18 into adult life. The extent to which care planning for and supporting permanence in foster care can create a family for life will rely on many features that interact between the child, the foster family, the birth family and the social work services.

Leaving care teams and services

One key aspect of the social work services that will be making a contribution to successful continuity of foster family life into adulthood will be the characteristics and expectations of the leaving care services (Sinclair, 2005). The groundbreaking work of Mike Stein and his colleagues in the 1980s (Stein and Carey, 1986) raised concerns that young people were leaving care unprepared and unsupported. As a result, the need for specialist teams to work with young people leaving care was accepted almost universally in social services departments and the significance of their work was confirmed by further research (for review see Stein, 2008), and recently reinforced by the Leaving Care Act 2004.

Although the development of both resources and expertise in the leaving care field was significant, necessary and valuable, some concerns have been raised in recent research (Schofield, 2003) that for children placed in long-term foster families there needs to be some flexibility in the way in which leaving care teams work with young people and their foster families, in particular, recognising that young people's sense of themselves may range from a temporary lodger to a child of the family. The routine pattern of being introduced at the age of 15 to a "leaving care" worker who may talk of being there to help with employment and accommodation when the young person leaves the foster home will be welcome to some, but will be unsettling to those in more settled and successful placements. As one 18-year-old, who had been in her long-term foster family since the age of nine, put it,

Why offer me a flat at 15 when I'm living in a family? It's only because I'm in care. I resent that. (Schofield, 2003)

In some interviews for this study it seemed that such concerns were being flagged up quite frequently by foster carers and social workers, but that the practice of leaving care teams was seen as unchallengeable.

In the survey, almost all local authorities (93%, 66) had separate teams which dealt with leaving care. These teams were most commonly called "leaving care teams" though some were called "after care" or "leaving and after care teams". A small number of local authorities, however, reported that they had recently been or were about to be reorganised in ways that would integrate "leaving care" workers into teams that were given titles such as adolescence teams, looked after children teams or adolescent looked after children teams. These changes were said to be happening in order to create continuity for young people and avoid the changeover of social workers at 16. There was some recognition that this might be a good idea for continuity – but also concerns that the special focus and expertise about older teenagers/care leavers might get lost and we could return to the days of the early 1980s when the special needs of care leavers were not sufficiently met. It was also feared, as with reorganisations generally, that this might actually turn out to be a cost-saving exercise which could lose resources for practitioners and care leavers – though it was too early to say if this would be the case.

The age at which local authority leaving care teams typically first get involved with a young person ranged from 13 to 16, with a mean age of 15. The age when the case transferred to the leaving care team ranged from 13 to 18 with a mean age of 16. The age of the child when the leaving care team was no longer involved ranged from 18 to 22, with a mean age of 21. There were no significant differences between single and dual systems, again suggesting that practice and procedures alongside planning for permanence remain quite similar, regardless of different terminologies and definitions.

As these figures suggest, leaving care workers may theoretically be involved with care leavers for up to nine years (i.e. age 13–22), including some who are in a long-term/permanent foster placements. The interview data showed that there were two different ways of structuring this involvement. The pattern for the majority of authorities was that after an introduction to the leaving care worker there was a (usually brief) period of overlap before case responsibility transferred to the leaving care team:

They become the child's social worker at 15½ or 16 depending on caseloads and people in post. The young person at 15½ will move to the Leaving and After Care Team, where they will have a new social

worker or personal adviser and they will move into that whole realm
of a kind of half adult world, I suppose. So it is a really big change at
a time when really they have got a huge number of other transitions
going on. (LAC, single)

Some practitioners felt that this change of worker at such a crucial time
(developmentally, socially and educationally) could be detrimental to the
child. In order to reduce the potential for stress and create a degree of
continuity, a few authorities extended the overlap period to a year or two
years rather than just a few months. However, there was some concern that
this longer transition meant that workload was increased, roles were
duplicated and the young person could become confused as to whom they
should turn to.

I have always felt you have a duplication of roles in some respects and
for it to continue for two years seems a long time to do a needs
assessment, which realistically tends to be done within six months and
is then updated as and when it needs to be. The Looked After Team
social worker still holds the case responsibility, so you quite often
have young people coming in, if they have got an issue that they want
to deal with, you know sort of everything gets pushed back to the
Looked After Team social worker to deal with first. (LAC, dual)

In order to avoid potential difficulties in the overlap period (no matter
how long or short), practitioners felt they had to plan roles and keep
communicating with each other:

As long as when you plan it or in the transfer planning meeting you
are very clear and precise about who is responsible for what, because
that is where it falls down, one says, 'Oh, I thought you were doing
that' and the other one says, 'No, no, I thought it was you!' But it has
now been integrated into our more general transfer protocol (LAC,
single)

An alternative service structure, as mentioned above, was to merge
the leaving care team with the looked after children's team so that a
child could potentially have the same social worker right up to and,

perhaps, beyond 18. This was often because the authority was small and they felt that having separate teams meant 'a lot of duplication, sometimes communication wasn't very good between the teams' (Fostering, single).

In more than one authority, the leaving care work was commissioned from a voluntary agency and young people would have advisers who took over the leaving care role.

The young persons' advisory service is commissioned out to [a voluntary organisation] . . . so the majority will eventually go over to the leaving care social worker but not all of them, some of them will remain with their social worker until they are 18. (LAC, single)

This kind of flexibility seemed unusual, but may enable children's different needs to be met.

Impact on young people of the leaving care service

The leaving care team's involvement appeared to be a requirement in all cases, regardless of the individual placement plan. As discussed in the definition section above, the goal was that many long-term/permanent placements would last beyond 18 and that placements would function like any other family. However, many practitioners believed that the involvement of the leaving care team at an early stage caused considerable anxiety in children and carers.

There is quite a fair degree of pressure on young people to think about living independently at that age, which of course most young people in a normal family situation would not necessarily be asked to do. They are still our children at that age, aren't they? So many foster carers would say and do say, that they feel that that is a pressure really for young people. At 16, to even begin to think about living more independently . . . and these are young people that have got greater needs and therefore might be less likely to move on and be ready for any kind of independent living. (Fostering, single)

A main theme in the focus groups was foster carers' view that the children in their care were not mature enough or able to look after themselves at age 18, let alone 16 or 17, the age at which some young people moved in to independence. Many carers made comparisons with non-foster families and claimed it was not expected there and yet the children they fostered were more vulnerable.

> *I think also it is around what children actually need once they reach the age of no longer being classed as a child. I think that is where the support is really needed and if you are a long-term carer, you can't just cut yourself off. Those children still need you as a resource. I think the average age of children leaving home is something like 26 across the country, but we are expecting children who have more difficulty by default to manage that transition at 18.* (Foster carer)

Practitioners suggested that children and carers thought that being asked to think about their future in such concrete terms was anxiety provoking and abnormal compared to families not within the care system. However, many reckoned that many young people would choose to move out of their foster home when they reach 18 and sometimes before.

> *They will stay, if they want to stay. But often it is the young person who will say, 'I want to go into my own accommodation' you know.* (Fostering, single)

Practitioners raised the issue that, unlike children in intact families outside of the care system, children in care hold more power than their caregivers over what happens in their future. Also, unlike most young people of their age, they have access to independent living. Practitioners suggested that young people often take up the offer of housing because, like many adolescents, they want their independence and want to try living without parental control. Some practitioners stated that because this option was available, the young people would take it up, even if it was not always the best course of action.

> *I think sometimes there is a tension in as much as an after care worker has it in mind that a young person has got some rights under the leaving care legislation of which they need to be advised. But if you said to my 17-year-old son, 'Well, if you decide to leave and move into independence, this is the flat you would get, etc.', he would wave*

'Tarra mother', pack his bag and leave. Because the grass is always greener on the other side. (Fostering, dual)

Although many young people said they wanted to leave care at an early age, staying until they were at least 18 was encouraged in some areas, with some success.

If a young person has been in foster care for a significant period of time, we would expect them to be staying there until they are . . . well, until they are 18. That doesn't mean that young people can't take themselves out of care and they often do, but you know that resources ought to be available to them until they are 18. (Fostering, dual)

It was noted by a couple of practitioners that *accommodated* children (CA 1989 s20) who did decide to leave care early could potentially lose all their leaving care entitlement.

If they are [under] s20 and leave foster care at 15 or 15½ and say 'I want to live with my mum', and by 16 it hasn't worked out, they have lost all their leaving and after care rights and so on. So they are very much on their own. Really vulnerable children, out there with no family. (LAC single)

Practitioners and carers were concerned that there were mixed messages around leaving care and long-term/permanent placements. Social workers and reviewing officers were expected to give the message to children and carers throughout childhood that the placement is a family until they become an adult and to assume commitment from both carers and children. But practitioners and foster carers commented that the involvement of the leaving care team contradicts this:

Permanence is permanence and it should be until the family system, the carer and the child are ready to say this is my time to move on. (Foster carer)

Some thought that the name "leaving care team" was anxiety provoking in itself and should be changed to something else.

The "leaving and after care team" – again it is very unfortunate terminology, isn't it? For somebody in a permanent placement it is scary. (LAC, single)

Many practitioners also recognised that the purpose of the leaving care teams was not just about where they were going to live in the future, but about preparing and helping them for life after school and getting them thinking about their future. They felt this should be promoted more to carers and young people, so that that becomes the focus rather then where they might live.

You know it is not about just where they are living and, in fact, for those that are in permanent placement, it is not about that at all. It may be about benefits, it may be about education, further education connections . . . and that should be made very clear. (Fostering, dual)

Communication between the leaving care team, the young person and the long-term or permanent foster carers

One difficulty that was recognised is that leaving care workers tend to have a particular agenda and way of working. Coming in at this point of transition, they often see themselves as befriender and advocate for the child. They expect to treat the child more like an adult than might previously have been the case. One of the consequences of this is that they may tend not to see the young person as a "child of the foster family" but as an independent adult. At its extreme, leaving care workers were said in one authority not even automatically to include the foster carer in pathway planning meetings, unless the young person requested them to be present. Up to that point (maybe 5–10 years) those foster carers have been expected to be active parents and are then treated as incidental to the young people's lives. In fact, concern shown by carers about young people is sometimes said to be an example of them being "overprotective" of their foster sons and daughters.

Fostering social workers described in interviews how long-term carers often felt anxious for the child at this stage, because they were not involved as much with or consulted by the leaving care worker as they had previously been by the child's social worker. They recognised that as well as redefining the role of the leaving care team in relation to long-term foster children, more could be done to ease anxiety by simply communicating with the carers and working together with them.

I think that there is some work for us to do in getting together the leaving and after care team and the foster carers so that they understand each other's roles . . . The focus of the work of the leaving and after care team is with the young people and sometimes the carers can feel out of the loop. It doesn't necessarily mean that the work is not being sensitively done, it is just that maybe the foster carers don't know how it is being done because they feel a little bit out of the loop and that is a problem for us here. (Fostering, single)

Some authorities recognised that communication was key to ensuring that carers did not feel anxious about the leaving care team's involvement and so offered training and support around leaving care. The emphasis here seemed to be more on providing a service to the family rather than taking over care of the child.

The leaving care team also provide training as well to foster carers. They come and bring everybody up to date with any changes and the support that is available. So I think you know everybody is aware of the services of the leaving care team and what is required and what is available, what support can be accessed. So I think it works quite well actually because everybody understands what is available, you know, good communication is the key here. (Fostering, single)

As with other areas of social work practice, it seems obvious that what is needed is a flexible approach to the work of the leaving care teams. There is some evidence that some leaving care workers did value and support the continuity for young people that might be available in the foster family. Their role in some cases will be active and central to the young person's transition, but in others their role will be to take a gentle and advisory back-seat, respecting the parenting role played by the foster carers. However committed the leaving care worker may be to getting alongside the child and offering support, it will be the foster family who may be able to offer Sunday lunch, Christmas dinner and become grandparents to the foster children's children.

Post-18 support and arrangements

Apart from the specific work of the leaving care teams, there were some more general concerns about arrangements for young people post 18. Many authorities wanted long-term/permanent placements to last beyond 18 and were concerned that they might not.

> *We would hope that when we agree matches for children for permanency that it will be for life, as it were, but legally it only has to be until the child reaches adulthood . . . Well, I think there is an ongoing issue really in terms of the quality of long-term fostering placements and the extent to which they can meet the child's needs, you know, for permanency and because of the very nature of fostering, which is that foster carers are not particularly obliged to continue caring for a child beyond the age of 18. There is always a concern as to how the child will be when they reach adulthood and will that family continue to have the same commitment to them.* (Panel Chair, single)

Continuity into adult life was said usually to occur when the relationship between the carers and young person was working very well and a sense of family membership had formed in the foster family.

> *Usually it is just a personal preference for them and the carers, you know. Carers want them to remain, they want to remain there. It is usually where they are very much part of the family and become settled . . . Usually if we have got to the point where they are there when they are 18, that is where they are planning to remain.* (LAC, single)

Practitioners often spoke about children returning to the foster family home on an informal basis long after they had left the family home.

> *Well, there is one young person who will . . . well, I think she is probably now 28, has her own children and has married, but is still in contact with her carer, the carer occasionally invites them to Sunday lunch. They have been involved in all the rites of passage, in terms of*

marriages and births and christenings and things like that. So there is that continuity; that will just go on for ever. (LAC, single)

This was also a recurring theme with most of the foster carers.

I'm there at the end of the phone, you know, they move on but they come back for Sunday dinner, they call me, all of my boys stay to dinner. (Foster carer)

Some practitioners said that some young people who had gone to university or college considered their foster family "home" and returned there in the holidays:

I can think of a case where we have got a kid who has gone off to university and they go back to the carers on an informal basis during the vacations. (LAC, single)

The financial support for this varied, with some authorities able to provide support for foster children while they were still in education:

They [leaving care] are certainly supporting people in university who are coming back to their placements. (Fostering, dual).

But other authorities provided very little support or only for a limited time:

We allow kids to stay in their permanent foster placements or current long-term placements while they remain in education up to the age of 19. (LAC, single)

Other arrangements post-18 included long-term/permanent placements turning into supported lodging placements to enable foster carers to still receive an income:

I think that children who are placed long term, quite often we find that foster carers are committed to them. When they get to 18 their placement transfers to supported lodgings, and that happens on many occasions, so it really is very long term. (IRO, single)

However, some practitioners stated that there were concerns for carers when long-term/permanent foster placements converted into supported lodgings schemes. Funding was reduced and the term "supported lodgings" should not be used to describe a family.

I have got one carer that said she felt really that as she had had the young person, she is 18 now, since she was nine, she found the change to supported lodgings really difficult herself. I mean, the young person doesn't, but she found it really difficult to think of her as a lodger in her home . . . She feels that she is not, she is far more to that young person than that and that the term sort of feels . . . yes . . . a bit derogatory. (Fostering, single)

What happened to children in long-term/permanent care at 18 appeared to be an important issue for many of the practitioners, with some stating that even though they wanted to build carer–child relations and create a family environment for the children, the children had the control and means to leave the placement early and there was no financial support offered for the most part to carers to care for children post 18. Many commented on *Care Matters* (Department for Education and Skills, 2007a) and were not sure how the recommendations regarding post-18 care would be implemented.

One of the things I would say is that we are getting distinct pressure on us from a lot of the independent fostering agencies and independent foster carers because of the comments in the Green Paper about children being able to remain with foster carers until they are 21. The interpretation of that is very varied, our view is that it means that they can stay living with them, but surely it can't be as a foster placement because once they are 18 they are no longer looked after. (LAC, single)

Nearly all practitioners stated that there were inadequate financial arrangements post-18 for children in long-term/permanent placements and this was reflected on by the foster carers too.

My oldest one is autistic. He has turned 18 and they actually cut all the finance off when he was aged 17 years, 364 days – at 18, you are getting nothing! You are getting nothing! (Foster carer)

If the financial situation is complicated and often unsatisfactory for young people and a local authority's own carers, there was also plenty of evidence of issues to resolve for young people and carers in the independent sector. In the survey and the focus groups it was clear that there were many concerns about the extent to which children in long-term or permanent IFP placements could rely on the local authority continuing to fund the placement into the late teens – and whether carers for whom fostering was often a career choice could continue to fund mortgages etc. while keeping a bedroom free for the "ex-foster child".

Such concerns add a degree of specific anxiety for IFP foster carers and for young people who may become aware of this risk to the future of a placement based on a financial contract that is beyond their control. But similar stresses can certainly occur for local authority carers. Whichever the provider, many young people need carers available into adulthood and this needs to be appropriately supported and funded.

6 Recruitment, preparation and approval of long-term and permanent foster carers

As with care planning and supporting children in placement, the research questions regarding the recruitment, preparation and approval of foster carers in this study focused on the extent and nature of practices specific to long-term and permanent care. Also, as with care planning, certain aspects of the process – the use of the Form F, for example – are regulated nationally and common to all foster care roles. So variations were likely to be local and perhaps difficult to track across agencies. However, some patterns did emerge in these areas of practice that seemed to reflect differences in approach to permanence in foster care and provide some ideas that might be useful for future investigation as models for practice.

General/specialist fostering teams and workers

The majority of local authorities, but the minority of IFPs, had separated out *foster carer recruitment* and *supervision* into separate teams. In our survey, 64 per cent (51) of local authorities and 36 per cent (24) of IFPs had separate workers and/or teams responsible for recruitment and supervision of foster carers. Significantly fewer IFPs had separate recruitment and supervision teams than local authorities,[14] with most commenting in the questionnaire that IFPs were often too small to warrant separate teams. There were no significant differences in practice structures between single and dual systems.

IFPs which had combined recruitment and supervision teams commented that, although this was often as a result of their size, there was also value in shared roles, expertise and continuity for social workers and also advantages in continuity for new foster carers.

Carers like the idea of their assessor becoming their supervising

---

[14] $\chi 2 = 10.81$, $df = 1$, $p<0.01$

social worker as this provides consistency and familiarity alongside the trust imported when completing the Form F. (Questionnaire, IFP)

However, shortages of the right kind of recruits for long-term and permanent foster care roles were mentioned by both IFPs and local authorities. The typical response to this dilemma from local authorities was that having separate recruitment teams was necessary and worked better on balance. It was reported that having a focused recruitment team or workers seemed to have increased the number of suitable foster carers for all roles joining the local authority. They also found advantages in having focused support and supervision teams which could respond more flexibly in a crisis if not tied, for example, to a carer training programme.

For these reasons, several practitioners from local authorities with joint teams mentioned that their local authority planned to develop specialist recruitment and supervision teams.

I think it needs somebody dedicated to recruitment which we don't have at the moment. I think that is where we are losing out to an extent. I have to say my authority doesn't have a huge problem with recruitment per se in that we have people ringing and enquiring every week about fostering. But, you know, finding the right kind of foster carers obviously is always the issue and all of our neighbouring authorities have a dedicated recruitment person. We are the only one that doesn't and we are the biggest authority and I think that is where we have a gap at the moment. (Fostering, single)

Enthusiasm for separate roles and teams was not universal in local authorities however. Some practitioners were concerned that if they separated out recruitment from supervision, the assessments would be less stringent and the carers potentially less suitable.

I think there is something specific about recruitment – but I also think there needs to be a sense of ongoing responsibility. For a very short time we did use independent people just to do our assessments and I think it bore out what I think we had feared anyway – which was that workers then don't have an investment in the people that they are recruiting and assessing in the way that they do when they know that they may well be supervising them. (Fostering, dual)

Implicit in this concern is that not only will the recruitment worker not be working with foster carers in the supervisory role, but they will also not be party to and responsible for placing children with those carers. Related concerns may be that where workers in recruitment teams either have not worked in a supervisory role previously or have moved into the recruitment team some time ago, they may be out of touch with current concerns and challenges for foster carers. This may then affect their judgement in assessment and the role they play in preparing carers.

It seems reasonable to suggest from this debate that, where there are separate teams, recruitment workers should keep in close touch with the supervisory teams, so that at the very least what happens to foster carers whom they have recruited – how they develop and grow in the role, the strengths and difficulties that may emerge after approval in the context of particular placements – can be fed back into the knowledge base of the recruitment team.

Some practitioners commented that they had a flexible approach to the organisation of recruitment and supervision within their fostering service. They suggested that these functions did not need to be formally split into teams, but that practitioners could choose the role which they felt best suited them within joint teams:

> We have an informal way of managing this. Everybody doesn't do everything – some people do more of what they are good at. So if we have got people who are good at assessments and really good at the turnover, they might do less support work and more assessments. (Fostering, single)

Further degrees of specialisation in relation to permanence were unusual. Only 20 per cent (16) of local authorities had specialist workers or teams who *specifically recruited long-term and permanent carers*. Almost a quarter of authorities with the single route (20%, 10) had specialist teams. Only one authority with the dual system stated that they had a separate team for long-term foster care (4%, 1) and five authorities with dual systems stated they had a separate recruitment team for permanent foster care (17%, 5). This low number of specialist recruitment workers and teams for permanence in foster care may reflect the fact that most placements with a permanence plan grow out of short-term placements and so the specialist work is in the reassessment of existing carers, normally carried out by supervising social workers. Then, perhaps, there is less need for a specialist recruitment team for permanence. On the other hand, given the overall shortage of placements for children needing a new foster care placement for permanence, the issue of whether specialist recruitment teams or workers might be helpful needs to be considered – or other arrangements made to ensure that both recruitment and supervisory teams are alert to identify carers who would be able to provide successful long-term/permanent placements.

The interview and questionnaire data suggested that in some cases where practitioners indicated that their local authorities had specialist teams for long-term/permanent foster care recruitment, they actually meant that the responsibility for recruiting, assessing and matching these foster carers had been transferred to the adoption family finding team. The decision had sometimes been taken to do this because a number of children had a parallel plan for adoption or foster care, because of their age or their needs, and so it was thought the potential new parents for these children should be recruited by the same team. They also felt that adoption teams had the right expertise for matching long-term/permanent foster placements.

> *The family finding function for long-term fostering will now be transferred to the adoption team. I think the experience of the adoption team, particularly through their management team . . . there is a huge amount of expertise in relation to matching child need and carer skill and ability and I think that will offer some improvement to how we do look at matching in long-term fostering.* (Fostering, single)

It is important to note here that this move towards using adoption-related personnel, expertise and procedures was only occurring on a small scale, but was happening in some local authorities with single systems for long-term foster care, not only dual system authorities promoting separate permanent foster care routes.

Recruitment policies regarding long-term and permanent foster carers

Policies regarding recruitment of foster carers for this task of providing permanence in foster care revealed a great deal about how the task itself was viewed. In particular, different local authorities and IFPs had quite different policies and approaches towards the *previous experience* a foster carer needed before they could care for a child on a long-term/permanent basis. Table 6.1 summarises local authority and IFP policies on new carers being approved as long-term or permanent foster carers with or without previous experience of fostering. It should be remembered that such "policies" may not be formally written down, but often exist at the level of custom and practice and reflect degrees of flexibility.

Table 6.1

Recruitment policy on allowing new carers to be approved as long-term/ permanent carers

Recruitment policy	Agency type	Single (LA n = 50, IFP n = 20)	Long-term dual (LA n = 32, IFP n = 46)	Permanent dual LA n = 30, IFP n = 38)
Carers do not have to be	LA	56%	66%	53%
task centred/short term first	IFP	35%	37%	34%
Some carers are approved	LA	34%	19%	27%
without being task centred/	IFP	25%	22%	16%
short term first – others are encouraged to be				
Carers are encouraged to be	LA	10%	13%	20%
task centred/short term first	IFP	15%	17%	21%
Carers are required to be	LA	0	3%	0
task centred/short term first	IFP	25%	24%	29%

There were no statistical differences between single and dual systems; however, there were statistically significant differences between local authorities as a group and IFPs. Over half of local authorities stated that long-term/permanent carers did not have to be task-centred/short-term foster carers first compared to about a third of IFPs.[15] While the figures are comparable in terms of *encouraging* applicants or *encouraging some* applicants to gain experience, almost no local authorities *required* applicants to gain experience compared to about a quarter of IFPs.[16] About a quarter of IFPs and authorities described themselves as having a flexible approach to recruitment in that they appreciated that some people would already have enough experience, either through caring for children informally or through their employment with children.

The importance of this question needs to be understood in the light of the fact that nearly all local authorities reported that most long-term/permanent carers were recruited from their in-house pool of carers anyway, rather than recruited new into the authority.

The majority of our permanent carers come from within our approved carer group, so when we are taking them back to panel it is for a change of approval from temporary short-term to long-term. (Fostering, dual)

Even so, most authorities would, in principle, allow new carers to care for a child on a long-term/permanent basis without any experience of caring for children short-term first. In the interview data practitioners stated that this arrangement can work well.

There are quite a few carers who come in and want to be long term carers and some of them are quite successful, even though they haven't fostered before. (Fostering, single)

Some practitioners were actively recruiting a small number of new carers specifically for the long-term/permanent role: 'I think our target for this year was five permanent foster carers' (Fostering, single). Practitioners mentioned, however, that people who came forward and were approved to foster long-term usually had experience of bringing up children or had worked with difficult children. They were therefore able to take a more flexible approach to recruitment.

---

[15] $\chi 2 = 10.91$, $df = 1$, $p<0.01$
[16] $\chi 2 = 30.04$, $df = 1$, $p<0.01$

I think it depends on the skills and competences of the carers. I mean, if I had a residential social worker coming forward who wanted to become a permanent foster carer, I am not going to send them away and say go and be a temporary foster carer first. It would depend. If it was a single carer who had never parented and had very little parenting experience, then you know we would question whether long-term fostering was right for them. On the other hand, if they came from a background in youth work, a single carer who had never parented but had a track record in working with extremely difficult adolescents, then we would assess them as a potential long-term carer. (Adoption and fostering, dual)

Of course, it is not unusual for long-term/permanent placements to evolve from the carers' first short-term placement i.e. they do not have previous experience of short-term caring in general, but find themselves in a first placement with a child to whom they feel they can make a long-term commitment. One local authority mentioned offering some carers "dual approval" so that they were able to care for children on either a short-term or long-term/permanent basis.

We are actually doing dual approval anyway – so we start off with task centred/long-term because some of our carers are quite keen to do both if they have got more than one placement to offer. (Fostering, single)

Other practitioners stated that their authorities were moving towards dual approval so that if placements became stable they could care for the child long-term without having to go back to panel and that these placements could be matched with that in mind from the start. The idea that children might be placed 'with a view to a long-term/permanent placement' – rather as in previous times children were placed 'with a view to adoption' – is quite controversial in the context of permanence planning and the need for clarity about placement goals. One viewpoint was that it is simply being realistic to place children who need long-term/permanent placements on a short-term basis with the hope or possibility that it could turn into a long-term/permanent placement. The testing out period can allow both carer and child to make an informed decision before committing to each other.

We will sometimes say to the carers – this is likely to need to be a long-term placement, but because you don't know this child and you are new to us, we are not necessarily asking you to make the commitment at this stage. Let's test it for three months and see how it goes. If it works, that is fine, you know, and we will think about making it permanent, but if it isn't working, there is no point in asking carers to commit to something that you know three months down the line is clearly going completely pear-shaped. (Fostering, dual)

This other practitioner, in contrast, was concerned that the notion of a trial period might cause drift and described how some children and young people can end up moving around the system.

What I feel concerned about is that we don't get into, you know, 'sale or return'. We may be looking for a family and the children live with one family and if that doesn't work out we move them on until we find a long-term family – or until they have reached an age when actually long-term families or permanent families will not be viable. (Fostering, dual)

Most authorities had a degree of flexibility across short-term and long-term roles in their approach to recruitment, but within that, a proportion did explicitly encourage some or all applicants to gain experience as short-term carers first. This was primarily because they felt that carers need to gain confidence in their ability to care for children in the care system and to understand what being a foster carer meant before they could make a commitment to a child on a permanent or long-term basis.

We tend to have more success recruiting permanent carers from within our existing group of carers. Once they know about the fostering system, they understand about the backgrounds of children and they have got an idea of what challenging behaviour actually means, rather than just talking about it theoretically, you know. They have got some experience behind them to actually be able to say yes, we know we can do this on a temporary basis and we want to make the commitment to it on a permanent basis. (Fostering, dual)

The position taken by rather more (though still a minority) of IFPs in relation to requiring previous experience also appeared to be in part a strongly-held belief that new foster carers needed to know more about the role, the difficulties of foster children and their own capabilities before committing themselves to a particular child.

> *Our experience is that foster carers need to show that they are able to commit to the care of other people's children and be resilient when placements are difficult before being considered for long-term or permanency.* (IFP questionnaire)

Some IFP practitioners even went as far as saying that it was "unsafe" for inexperienced carers to care for children long-term:

> *We consider this to be a fundamental requirement. It is unsafe to place children on a long-term basis with inexperienced carers.* (IFP questionnaire)

Some IFPs had clear policies on this and had put in place training plans to mark the necessary progression up to becoming carers for the agency.

> *Our carers move through a sequence whereby they are registered as sessional carers, then approved as respite carers and then move on to full-time care approval. They may choose to remain in one of the former stages. This process means that carers gather experience in managing behaviours and gather experience in a controlled and monitored manner.* (IFP questionnaire)

However, other IFP practitioners commented that the policy of requiring carers to gain short-term caring experience first was flawed and that many first placements evolved into long-term/permanent placements anyway. 'The [policy] is not too practical; we have had new carers take a child as a first placement who never went home' (IFP questionnaire). Some believed that prospective carers should be treated on an individual basis, 'We believe that each applicant is different, some are clearly long-term permanent carers' (IFP questionnaire), and that rigid policies were restricting, 'If we had hard and fast rules about this our carers would never start caring' (IFP questionnaire). Those who would place children on a long-term/permanent basis with carers without experience stated that whether the placement would work 'depends on matching' and the assessment needed to be of high quality and then 'rigorously questioned at panel'.

But one IFP pointed out that their more restrictive policy arose to some extent from a belief that for a local authority to commit a child (and the attendant finance) to a permanent placement in an IFP, they would need reassurance in the form of evidence that the carers had the necessary experience and skills.

In discussing the role of prior experience, practitioners raised the important issue of the comparison between recruitment of long-term/ permanent foster carers and recruitment of adoptive parents, where it is common for adoptive parents to commit life-long to a child without previous parenting experience. Some felt that if adoption could work in those circumstances, then there was no reason why carers should not be recruited to care for children long-term.

If you want to draw a comparison . . . often couples who have never had children of their own are approved as adopters, so you know as long as they have had access to training and there is going to be appropriate support, then why not? (LAC, single)

However, other practitioners stressed that the role was completely different to adoption in that, as above, foster carers had to learn to work with social services, manage regular and sometimes frequent contact and handle more challenging child behaviour. Indeed, this was also a point brought up by several foster carers:

I mean, when you are a foster carer, the most challenging parts to your role I find are working with the system. When you are an adopter you don't have to do that at all. (Foster carer)

In the foster carer focus groups, the importance of previous fostering experience divided opinion – in one group quite dramatically. For this group, which had agreed over most other aspects of their roles, the question, 'Do you think long-term carers need to have been short-term carers first?' polarised the group, with instant responses – 'Of course they do!' and 'Of course they don't!'

These different responses seemed to be associated with two rather different approaches and foster family experiences represented in the focus group. Although all members of the group were very committed to their children as part of the family who would remain with them through to adulthood, there seemed to be differences in their perceived role as a foster carer for their agencies. Carers who felt that it was fine to become a long-term foster carer first had more commonly taken a single child or sibling group and this had completed their family. This may have been a first family or a second family, where carers had grown up birth or previous foster children. They valued social work support as foster carers and promoted contact with birth families, but seemed to see themselves in some respects as more like adopters with settled families. They were not, for example, looking to take more children or to play other roles.

In contrast, carers who felt that it was essential to have short-term experience first were more likely to emphasise the "professional" role that they played, to have more diverse fostering backgrounds – perhaps combining short-term and long-term placements, perhaps offering respite care, caring for disabled children who needed a lot of professional attention. Alongside their professional commitment to their carer role, they gained satisfaction from their informal and extensive families (including former foster children) and one carer described a full house for Sunday lunch: 'The Sunday lunch gets bigger and bigger in our house; yesterday there were fourteen of us!'. They had very flexible family boundaries and included many children but they also valued their professional role with regard to the agency; for example, offering training and support to other carers, campaigning for carers and so on.

From this simple typology one might question whether there was a pattern in terms of agency – were certain types of carers more likely to be from local authorities or from IFPs? In fact, there was strong representation in both groups from local authority carers and IFP carers. This was a very valuable lesson. It was perhaps not so surprising that the full range was represented among local authority carers, but it was important to note that families seeking to build a new family or have a second family now that older children are grown up are very much part of the IFP profile. This makes it interesting that IFPs were statistically less likely to accept new carers for permanence than local authorities – but perhaps justifies the development of IFPs which specialise in providing permanent placements.

Such distinctions in attitudes and identities become relevant when we look back to agency definitions and expectations of foster carers, but are also relevant when we consider both the qualities of foster carers (below) and attitudes to taking legal steps to secure permanence through adoption or special guardianship (Chapter 8).

Long-term and permanent foster carer qualities

In considering recruitment, preparation and approval of carers in the context of permanence, it seemed important to test out whether different agencies would offer different accounts of what qualities they were looking for. The question as to which qualities make foster carers best able to provide successful long-term and permanent foster care produced very full and interesting comments on the survey questionnaire and also led to revealing discussions in the telephone interviews.

Qualities fell broadly into four dimensions, which were mentioned by all agencies – local authorities and IFPs. Some aspects of each dimension were common to all foster care roles, but other aspects were thought of as particularly relevant to defining the task of offering permanence. These four dimensions were the carers' commitment and skills in respect of:

- meeting the child's developmental needs through to adulthood;
- providing family membership for the child through to adulthood;
- working constructively with the child's birth family through to adulthood;
- working constructively with social workers and other agencies on behalf of the child through to adulthood.

Although there were distinctions made by some agencies between the qualities of permanent carers and those of long-term carers, mainly in relation to the concept of family membership (which will be discussed below), even dual system authorities would most often state that the nature of the commitment and the importance of this commitment and associated skills were very similar in both types of placement plan.

Commitment and skills to meet the child's developmental needs through to adulthood

The commitment and capacity to meet the child's developmental needs was required in the short, medium and longer term through to adult life. This had to be founded on a good understanding of the child's history and its consequences for the child's current and future behaviours, relationship strengths and difficulties. There was said to be a range of children's developmental needs that would have to be met with significant commitment from carers, including additional health and educational needs.

More detailed accounts of what qualities and skills might help carers in this process of supporting the child's development included the following: being child-centred and seeing children as individuals; accepting and valuing difference and diversity; being able to express empathy and sympathy for children and their family situations; being patient; having the ability to exercise good parental control; having clear expectations but being non-judgemental; having a sense of humour and enjoying children; being able to reflect and continue to learn; being an effective advocate; being enthusiastic and pro-active. Some factors were seen as linked to these carer qualities – for example, having had experiences of working through difficult periods in their own life, viewing these experiences positively and having good support networks in the family and the community. Here was a fairly typical list of qualities from one social worker.

> *Characteristics of long-term foster carers include commitment to the child; the ability to form and sustain long-term mutually supportive relationships with adults and children; an ability to accept children for who and what they are in order for them to achieve their full potential; an ability to manage challenging behaviour by setting safe, clear and consistant boundaries; a good understanding of child development and issues of attachment, separation and loss; good communicators and advocates for children. They need to be flexible, accommodating, warm, caring, nurturing, resourceful, reliable and honest.* (Questionnaire, fostering, single)

With specific relevance for permanence, the most commonly mentioned relationship qualities were linked to helping the child to build a secure attachment to the foster carers. Not surprisingly, therefore, the most commonly mentioned problem for carers to understand from children's histories was the difficulty most children with insecure attachments and experiences of abuse, loss and moves had in committing themselves to new families. It was here that social workers would mention specifically the foster carers' ability to cope with few rewards and slow progress in the early stages of a placement – to the point of accepting that, although they as carers needed to commit fully to the relationship, the child may never fully reciprocate.

On this theme, several related issues emerged around what was commonly termed "stickability" or resilience. For many social workers, this was first on the list of necessary qualities. In what was inevitably a context of concerns about trying to anticipate and prevent the breakdown of planned long-term and permanent placements, practitioners emphasised the importance of foster carers being able to stick with children though the difficult times; times when they might feel like giving up but would find a way to cope, survive and often become stronger as a result. This capacity was seen as likely to arise from a combination of the personal and parenting qualities listed above *and* experience of caring for troubled children. In particular "stickability" was seen as necessary in order to handle the potential challenges of the adolescent years, when clearly social workers felt additional concerns about the viability and continuity of placements which had been set up when children were quite young.

Commitment and skills to provide family membership for the child through to adulthood

Also specific to long-term and permanent placements, a key quality looked for in foster carers was said to be a strong commitment to welcoming the child as a full member of the foster family. This was universally stressed as important from the start of a planned placement, but was seen as particularly important in terms of the commitment to treat the child as part of the family through to adulthood – and beyond.

One or two respondents suggested that foster carers needed to understand that they were not the child's parents – but for most, the possible taking on by carers of the role of parents was perhaps sidestepped in favour of an emphasis on the language of providing family membership. Here, distinctions were made mainly between short-term/ task-centred foster care and long term/permanent foster care. Comparisons with adoption, where parenthood is explicit, were not made, but nevertheless, the overall expectation of carers being able to build secure attachment, promote a child's development and offer full family membership into adult life was comprehensive and not dissimilar to adoption.

The family membership dimension in particular was stressed by foster carers in all three focus groups as the key to permanence in foster care. They described how important it was for them – and how important they believed it to be for their children – to feel that their foster home was a fully committed and inclusive family, a "real family" rather than a "placement". They talked passionately about their roles as families in loving, advocating for and supporting children through thick and thin, as they would their birth children.

Commitment and skills to work constructively with the child's birth family through to adulthood

However forcefully the case was put for foster family membership, it was also expected that successful foster carers would need to be able to work constructively with birth families and to maintain as far as possible the child's relationship with the birth family through childhood and adolescence. As with other dimensions, this required the right attitude, or "commitment", as well as relevant "skills". The message here was that foster carers needed to be both empathic and accepting of birth parents and able to take practical steps, for example, in terms of facilitating contact, to help children manage their two families.

The importance of birth families was also reflected in the foster carer focus groups, where carers who talked so passionately about the foster child's place in their family also talked passionately about the child's right and need to have appropriate contact with birth family members. One carer described how the local authority had reduced their child's contact with key birth family members, such as grandparents, in order to protect the "permanence" of the placement. She felt strongly – and had argued with social workers – that far from protecting the placement, the lack of contact was actually making the child feel sad and preoccupied. In the same focus group, however, another carer talked about getting to know the birth parents over time and bringing them to a shared recognition that the frequency of contact in this case was actually too much for the child – and negotiating a reduction in contact, in the context of the birth parents' increased trust in the foster carer.

The role of foster carers in decisions relating to work with birth parents and contact were discussed above (see Chapter 5), but it is clear from social workers and carers that working with birth parents was an essential part of securing both the quality of the child's experience and the stability of the placement in the longer term. (There is a lack of research on working with birth parents of children in long-term foster care. An ESRC funded project at UEA, led by Gillian Schofield in collaboration with parallel projects in Norway and Sweden, is currently addressing this issue and will report in 2009.)

Commitment and skills to work constructively with social workers on behalf of the child

There was universal agreement that foster carers needed to be able to work constructively with social workers (and other professionals) if children were to thrive and placements were to be stable. This quality in relation to working with social workers was often described as 'being good at working in a team', and it was obviously hoped that teamwork was the spirit of this relationship. However, it was recognised that the responsibility of social workers to scrutinise the work of foster carers as well as support them, and to oversee and promote the well-being of foster children, means that foster carers need to accept a degree of professional scrutiny alongside the help and resources that they or the children might seek and need.

The working relationship with social workers in relation to permanence was very clearly highlighted in the recognition by practitioners, and indeed foster carers in the focus groups, that the balance between the "parenting" responsibilities of carers and of social workers does shift in situations where the decision has been made for a child to grow to adulthood in this foster family. As is known from other studies (Beek and

Schofield, 2004a; Thoburn *et al*, 2000) and accounts of foster family life (Cairns, 2004), it is quite possible for foster family life to be managed in ways that enable the child to feel at home and part of the family, while the procedural requirements and support and monitoring functions of corporate parenting are observed. But in terms of assessing, preparing and supporting foster carers to walk this line, it was recognised that this dimension was an area that needed to be explored very carefully. In summary, as one practitioner helpfully put it:

> *No carer is going to have all the characteristics outlined and where gaps are identified these need to be addressed through training, supervison and support, including peer support.* (Questionnaire, fostering, dual)

The message from these lists of qualities is that they can be very useful in the process of assessing, preparing and supporting foster carers. They can help to identify strengths, but also to identify areas where more support and training will be needed over the years of the placement.

Methods used to recruit long-term and permanent carers

Even though practitioners commented that most of their long-term/ permanent carers were recruited from their pool of short-term carers, some authorities and IFPs used recruitment methods specifically to attract new carers to care for children on a long-term/permanent basis as shown (Figure 6.1). Recruitment methods which seemed to be used most by authorities were websites and children's profiles.

Websites

The vast majority of local authorities (98%, 79) and IFPs (91%, 60) had a website which potential carers could access. Seventy-seven per cent (59) of authorities and 32 per cent (20) of IFPs reported having specific information about long-term or permanent foster care on their website. This difference between authorities and IFPs was statistically significant.[17] IFPs perhaps used methods such as websites for recruiting

---

[17] $\chi2 = 23.38$, $df = 1$, $p<0.01$

Figure 6.1
Recruitment methods for long-term/permanent foster carers

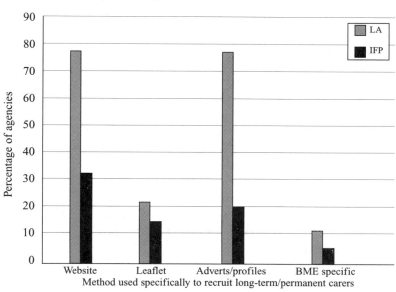

long-term and permanent carers less than local authorities, because they less commonly wanted new carers to offer long-term permanent placements. There were no statistical differences between single and dual systems in terms of use of websites.

Opinion in the survey questionnaire and interviews varied considerably about how well websites worked in terms of recruiting long-term/ permanent carers. Some practitioners doubted their success.

Long-term fostering is part of the information included in the website; but there is no evidence that the website has generated much tangible response. (Questionnaire, fostering, single)

Others felt that the website was a helpful source of information:

It works well; people can consider different options and what they would like to do at an early stage of application. (Questionnaire, fostering, dual)

Although in a minority, nearly all of the IFPs which included information on long-term foster care spoke in praise of their website: 'It seems to send the right sort of carers our way' (IFP). Practitioners from one local authority included in the interviews also spoke very positively of their website. They believed that it had generated a large number of enquiries for all types of foster carers, because it allowed easy access to information. Many of the comments in the questionnaire indicated that their websites were in need of updating. However, this authority regularly updated their information:

> *The reason it works particularly well is that we have got the website on all of the adverts we run, wherever we run them, and you know, I think that many more people will go onto the computer and check it out. We have got lots of links with other agencies and we have hyperlinks across to all the advertising I do with the large newspaper chains. It works extremely well for us. I think also because people can apply online for a pack of information – it is just so much quicker.* (Fostering, dual)

As this quotation suggests, marketing strategies and sophisticated uses of technology are now very much part of the recruitment of foster carers, but do require skills that are not the usual social work skills, so that marketing experts are sometimes employed for this work.

Leaflets

Only a few local authorities (21%, 17) and IFPs (14%, 9) had leaflets which were specific to long-term or permanent foster care as shown in Figure 6.1. The difference between local authorities and IFPs was not statistically significant, nor were there any statistical differences between single and dual systems.

As with the websites, comments varied on how useful practitioners felt specific leaflets on long-term/permanent fostering were. Some practitioners felt that specific leaflets were counter-productive at the recruitment stage because they would confuse potential carers when they were just becoming familiar with the meaning of foster care.

> *Specific leaflets are not necessary as, at the initial stages, prospective*

carers seldom know what they want. It is part of the assessment to explore. (Fostering, single)

Some practitioners believed that specific leaflets were useful even quite early in the recruitment and assessment/preparation process, because they allowed potential foster carers to start to think about what they would like their role to be.

Recruiting specifically for long-term/permanent carers produces more focused response from potential applicants. (Fostering, dual)

One practitioner reported that, rather than having leaflets about the different types of foster care, they produced leaflets based on the age of child: 'a specific leaflet for a child 8+, which raises the need for long-term foster carers is in use' (Fostering, single). This is interesting practice as it places the needs of the child in the forefront of the potential carer's mind.

Advertisements and profiles

The majority (77%, 62) of local authorities used advertisements or profiles to recruit long-term or permanent foster carers for specific children, compared to only 20 per cent (13) of IFPs. This difference was statistically significant.[18] It is the local authority's duty to find carers for specific children and therefore they are responsible for advertising. Where IFPs mention that they had used specific advertisements, some had responded to an advertisement rather than placed one, or they may have been given permission by the authority to include profiles in recruitment literature.

In response to a number of long-term referrals for a particular age group of young people, our adverts will have a theme to recruit carers that will match against the referrals received. (IFP, questionnaire)

Some practitioners commented in the questionnaires and interviews that featuring children's profiles in the local press generated enquiries, including some suitable potential long-term/permanent foster carers.

---

[18] $\chi2 = 41.69$, $df = 1$, $p<0.01$

We put out those adverts, like you do when you want adoptive families for children. So we put a pen picture about that child and what we are looking for. So then we get people who phone in specifically for those children or young people. Then some have further discussion. They might say well, actually, no we are not right for those children, but we are still interested in others. We have successfully recruited foster carers following a recruitment advert... Actually, as a result of adverts we have probably recruited four families as a result of featuring ten pictures of children, so it can work. (Fostering, single)

However, the majority suggested that featuring children in the local press had not been very successful, because the enquirers were not suitable and had not resulted in many children being placed.

Adverts for a specific child in the local press are very rarely successful. They may generate general enquiries, but do not usually lead to a specific match. (Questionnaire, fostering, dual)

Some practitioners felt that advertisements in fostering publications had been more successful, but these enquiries were usually from their own carers or the independent sector.

When you advertise in local papers and things like that, it is probably not necessarily that successful. If you are using something like, you know, the Fostering Network's Family Finders, then you will get a lot of responses because often they may not necessarily come from the adults themselves, they might come from the actual fostering agency. (Fostering, single)

Two authorities mentioned that information evenings featuring profiles which were open to prospective foster carers and adopters as well as existing foster carers were successful.

We hold a project evening where profiles, videos and DVDs are presented of children/young people needing permanency, whether this be permanency via adoption or fostering. These have been very successful for some children. (Questionnaire, LAC, single)

It is clear that, while there is some ambivalence about whether foster carers should be approved initially as long-term carers or take on a child with a plan for permanence as a first placement, the role of specific and targeted recruitment strategies may be valuable for some carers but also has some limitations. On the other hand, certain approaches, e.g. special sections on a website, may still be highly cost effective in setting out the full range of fostering and in generating interest.

Recruitment campaigns for black and minority ethnic (BME) carers

Rather more local authorities, 43 per cent (35) than IFPs, 27 per cent (17), had recruitment campaigns aimed at BME groups, but this difference was not statistically significant. Eleven percent (9) had specific information about long-term or permanent foster care, as did five per cent (3) of IFPs. This difference was not significant. The questionnaire comments indicated a mixture of success with some stating they had moderate success; 'numbers have risen by two in the last year' (Questionnaire, fostering, single)

Perhaps surprisingly, this question did not generate much comment, so it is unclear whether the general recruitment of BME carers to take children with long-term/permanent plans was satisfactory or not.

Preparation of foster carers

The great majority of authorities and IFPs used a general preparation for approval course which included material on long-term/permanent foster care rather than a specialised course, as shown in Table 6.2. There were no statistical differences between authorities and IFPs or between single and dual systems. Only a very small minority of authorities (5%, 4) and IFPs (11%, 7) had separate preparation courses for long-term or permanent carers. Most authorities stated that a separate preparation course was not viable due to the very small number of prospective carers that approach the authorities to become long-term/permanent foster carers; 'Numbers are too low to run a separate course' (Questionnaire, fostering, dual). Some practitioners thought that a separate preparation course would be unhelpful, because new carers should learn about all aspects of fostering, as they may well take children for various lengths of time and for various tasks.

Many foster carers have mixed placements so are using new knowledge in a much wider framework and this is more relevant to them. (Questionnaire, fostering, single)

However, a number of practitioners stated that if people were coming forward for long-term/permanent foster care, the preparation should be more focused because the task is so different to being a task-centred carer and that carers need to learn different skills:

I think they are two very different tasks and therefore preparing someone for children who come and go is a different task to preparing somebody for looking after a child and, you know, being clear that when this child comes to live with you, this is where they are coming to stay. (Fostering, dual)

One IFP (an approved adoption agency) stated that carers looking to do long-term/permanent work would also do the adoption training:

We provide additional training for permanent carers on fostering issues – most attend the adoption training which has relevant topics such as attachment, life story work, abuse, safe caring etc. (IFP questionnaire)

A small minority of authorities and IFPs had training which focused on short-term foster care and did not include information about long-term/permanent foster care. Interestingly, these same authorities did allow people to be long-term/permanent carers with no prior experience. One authority, which provided task-centred training, commented: 'More specific prep is needed' (Questionnaire, fostering, dual). However, most of the other practitioners from authorities with task-centred focused preparation stated they offered additional training to carers who were interested in fostering long-term/permanently: 'We would offer further training for carers if required to do long-term' (Questionnaire, fostering, single) or long-term/permanent foster care was discussed during assessment: 'Permanence issues are focused on during assessment' (Questionnaire, fostering, dual).

Only seven (9%) local authorities and two (3%) IFPs provided preparation specific to BME carers. Similarly, a small number (9, 13%) of local authorities and two (4%) IFPs provided preparation material in a non-English language (most typically London Boroughs, Midlands and Welsh authorities).

Table 6.2

Focus of the preparation course

	Agency type	Single (LA n = 50, IFP n = 21)	Long-term dual (LA n = 32, IFP n = 45)	Permanent dual (LA n = 28, IFP n = 40)
Preparation course focussed on short-term	LA	12%	16%	14%
	IFP	19%	13%	15%
General preparation course including material focused on long-term/permanent	LA	84%	81%	79%
	IFP	67%	78%	75%
Separate courses for long-term permanent carers	LA	4%	3%	7%
	IFP	14%	9%	10%

The task of becoming a permanent carer has a number of components – as we saw in considering the special qualities that are needed and need to be promoted in foster carers. Many of those qualities – from resilience and sensitivity to the child's needs, to working with birth parents and social workers – are common to other forms of foster care, but with the important addition of family commitment through into adult life. So it is a matter of ensuring that, through processes of preparation and post-approval training, these qualities are recognised, developed and sustained.

Foster carer approval

Given the range of agency differences already identified, it was not surprising to find that different authorities also had different approaches to approving long-term and permanent carers. However, here the differences were minor, with the fostering panel used by most authorities and IFPs in approving long-term/permanent foster carers, especially where there was no change to the placement other than a change of status. For permanent foster carers in the dual system, whether new to the authority or being approved as long-term/permanent for a child, there was a slight trend for the adoption and permanent panel or the adoption panel to be used by more authorities. The few IFPs who used an adoption and permanence panel were agencies which provided adoptive placements too. Around 10 per cent of authorities did not re-approve existing carers (LT 9%, 6; P 11%; 4).

As with best interests and matching, a combination of panels was used by some local authorities (just under 5%) with, typically, carers being approved for younger children going to a permanence or adoption and permanence panel and carers being approved for older children going to the fostering panel.

Approval of family and friends carers as long-term or permanent foster carers occurred at the fostering panel for the vast majority (S 83%, 40; LTD 81%, 21; PD 77%, 17), with the remaining local authorities approving friends and family carers at the permanence panel, adoption and permanence panel or a combination.

One problem specific to IFPs was that sometimes they had approved the carer, but there could be delays with the local authority in matching in existing placements.

> *However, once approved as a permanent carer, we then need to go to local authority for a match – this can take a very long time – nearly two years in two cases!!!* (Questionnaire, IFP)

Most practitioners felt that the fostering panel was the most appropriate place to approve carers as long-term/permanent carers, especially as many of them had already been approved as task-centred carers.

> *That is what the fostering panel is set up for – to approve all and anybody who wants to foster for [local authority]. They approve short-term, long-term, permanent and families who are doing respite care, family link, and perhaps short breaks for children with disabilities. My understanding is that they have reviewed that and the current system works well and the carers understand it.* (Fostering, dual)

Some local authorities used different panels for approval and matching. Practitioners from authorities which used the fostering panel for approval and the adoption and permanence panel or permanence panel for matching, generally felt the system worked well and there were usually no problems, although they could highlight one or two difficult cases:

> *All foster carers start off going through the fostering panel and it is when you are then linking to a particular child that it then goes to the adoption panel. It is difficult really, because I think sometimes there has been a lack of understanding between the two. But I think things have improved and the Chairs meet regularly . . . I think the adoption panel sometimes raise the issue of 'why not adoption' which is fair enough, I think, to consider what is the best permanence plan.* (Fostering, single)

Perhaps in recognition of the importance of asking the question of why not adoption at an earlier stage, several local authorities took child best interest decisions for long-term/permanent foster care to the adoption panel, but the carer approval and matching decisions were made at the fostering panel.

Documentation used for existing long-term and permanent foster carer approval

The question of documentation is not merely one of procedure – it raises questions about the type of assessment and the range and quality of information available to decision makers, it reflects the way in which permanence in foster care is viewed, and it provides comparisons with adoption.

Documentation required for approval of new foster carers includes a completed Form F and full medical report. However, for approval of existing carers who become long-term/permanent carers, local authorities and IFPs vary in the level of further assessment and type of paperwork they required. As shown in Table 6.3, almost all local authorities and IFPs required an updated Form F to approve carers as long-term or permanent who had been previously approved as short-term or task centred. More often than not this included extra or new references. Under half of the local authorities and IFPs required an updated medical report. Those that did not require it stated that they relied upon the latest medical report, 'unless there is a change in health. Otherwise medicals are every two years as per BAAF recommendations'. (Questionnaire IFP)

Table 6.3
Documentation used for existing long-term and permanent foster carer approval

Documentation	Agency type	Single (LA n = 48, IFP n = 19)	Long-term dual (LA n = 24, IFP n = 38)	Permanent dual LA n = 24, IFP n = 34)
Updated Form F	LA	90%	83%	92%
	IFP	95%	90%	91%
Updated Medical Report	LA	47%	42%	50%
	IFP	26%	38%	52%

This picture on the whole does suggest that carers who are continuing to care for a child, but with a change of plan to long-term or permanent, are subject to further assessment. The detail and quality of this assessment may vary, but systems appear to be in place to mark the change of role and undertake some sort of "matching" process.

Providing a choice of long-term and permanent placements

It is obviously desirable to have a choice of foster carers available if a good match is to be made for an individual child or sibling group, although the notion of a number of approved foster carers being "available" (i.e. without the approved number of children already placed or the accompanying income) is clearly difficult to manage in any system. However, some practitioners stated that they did have some placement choice, at least some of the time, for children in need of long-term/ permanent foster care and were able to match properly.

We are looking for a long-term placement for two children at the moment and we do actually have some placement choice. (Fostering, single)

However, more commonly, practitioners stated that finding suitable long-term/permanent placements was a challenge.

We have always got more children waiting for long-term placements than we have got long-term placements. (LAC, single)

There was widespread concern that children might simply be placed with any available carer. Practitioners commented that they often could not do proper matching because of foster carer shortages.

They are in desperate need of more foster carers, so there isn't much matching done. If a child goes to a family and they eventually decide that the care plan is going to be long term and that family can only look after that child short term, a referral will be made to the fostering team who have weekly meetings to appropriately match children. For instance, we have a lot of the children who can't be with younger children, and some children who are abusers and can't be with other children. So there is that kind of matching that goes on, but they also look for foster carers who are able to take children long term who aren't short-term carers. But we do have quite a number of those who say they don't want long term . . . they like a turnover of children. (IRO, dual system)

This anxiety about the absence of matching was also a theme with foster carers. Some carers reported having had children placed with them on a long-term/permanent basis, even though they were approved for a different type of child and fostering role, because of a lack of other available placements.

Myself and my husband were passed through panel in July last year as short-term carers for children up to age eleven. Then in September they rang us about a 13-year-old child who needed long-term care. So she was our first child and she was long-term. (Foster carer)

As has already emerged in earlier discussions, practitioners said that most of the children in long-term/permanent placement had been placed with their long-term/permanent carer on a short-term basis and it was later decided that the children should remain there on a long-term/permanent basis, rather than being in a placement which was previously matched through assessment. The question of *choice* and *matching* for long-term placement thus relates in many cases to whether this placement is good enough to meet the child's needs in the longer term, a decision which most local authorities take back to a meeting or panel. However, that assessment and judgement of whether the existing placement is good enough is to some extent going to be influenced by the availability of other, preferable, placements. The panel may take a similar or different view of the current placement, but their scrutiny is useful in avoiding both delayed and rushed decisions.

Most practitioners reported that placements which evolved from short term to long term often work best, because the carers know and are committed to the child, there is already evidence that the placement is working well and the child is in agreement, regardless of whether they were previously matched.

> *The most successful long-term placements we have over the years are the ones where task-centred carers have said, 'I wish to keep this young person long term' and that young person has made that choice as well and they are the most enduring.* (Fostering, single)

This was also reiterated in the foster carer focus groups, with plenty of examples of placements which had evolved out of short-term placements and worked well:

> *We started off as short term and our first placement were the girls, five and eight. The plan was to go back to mum and, if that didn't work out, then the next plan was adoption. But though people were coming in wanting to adopt the younger girl, because the older one has disabilities, nobody wanted to adopt her. The court stated that they must stay together because there were only the two of them at the time. Now the adoption didn't happen because of that reason so the next plan was long-term [fostering] and by then we had had them about two years, two to three years, and we were asked would we be able to have them on a long-term basis – which we were so pleased we were asked because we'd started to work with them.* (Foster carer)

Other research (Schofield *et al*, 2000) also reports this sense that foster carers have of starting to 'work with' children and invest in them, before the long-term plan is made. But then when the plan is made, carers feel relief to know that not only will they continue to be able to promote the children's development, but that they, as well as the children, will see the benefits and reap the rewards of this investment of time, energy and love.

One challenge for practice in linking children and new families must be how – when the plan is still uncertain – to link children with families who would be appropriate to keep them if or once the plan is confirmed. This is not quite the same as a "trial period" though it does have some of the risk and benefits of that practice in terms of uncertainty. But hopefully, the uncertainty here is weighted in favour of the child being able to stay because, in principle at least, a long-term placement with this family would not have been ruled out at the start and may prove to be a positive option. This is perhaps more appropriately seen as a variation on concurrent planning in adoption – although these are older children with uncertain behaviours and views of their own.

Some practitioners felt that their authorities should actively encourage more formal early matching to take place for long-term/permanent placements, so that the focus was on meeting the needs of the child rather than suiting the carers' wishes.

I would get more matching taking place earlier to help build the stability of the placement and so that the focus is on the needs of the child. Whereas I think sometimes we can get hooked up in terms of the carer saying, 'Oh well, I am interested now' rather than thinking 'Oh, just hang on a minute, what are the needs of the child here? How does this foster carer meet those needs?' (LAC, single)

Because of shortages of long-term foster carers, and the general anxiety about moving a child, the tendency to sigh with relief when a carer says they will keep a child is very understandable. Social workers were very aware of this risk and it almost certainly contributed to their favouring the use of the independent scrutiny of the match by fostering or adoption panels, so that the appropriateness of the placement could have additional investigation and independent confirmation.

In investigating recruitment and matching of long-term/permanent carers with particular children, the question arose as to *whether carers do or should continue to play other fostering roles*, either roles that they may wish to play or that the local authority would like them to play. Nearly all local authorities (and IFPs) said that it was possible for long-term/permanent carers to provide task-centred placements, for example, as well as other types of placement (S 100%, 50; LTD 100%, 31; PD 93%, 28). But all maintained, also, that it was always important to assess the foster family circumstances before making this decision, taking into account the feelings of birth, fostered and adopted children in the foster family, as well as the needs of the specific child. These assessments and decisions call for difficult professional judgements and both local authorities and IFPs were clearly having to negotiate carefully with carers to make sure that families were not overburdened or that existing long-term or permanent placements were not threatened by the arrival of newcomers. At times, it is foster carers who want to take on too much, but at other times, it is social workers who are persuading carers to take more children when perhaps caring for just one very needy child may be right for the child and the foster family.

One consequence of carers becoming long-term carers, whether for an existing child or a child new to them, was that if carers cared for a child in a long-term/permanent placement they would be "out of circulation" for other types of placement.

> *The very fact of making a long-term or permanent placement – what you are doing is taking that foster carer out of circulation for the next five, six, ten or whatever years. So although you have created an excellent resource for that particular child, often if you are converting a short-term or temporary placement into a long-term or permanent placement, you have taken away a resource from the children who need temporary and short-term placements to create one for a child that needs a permanent placement. So although that is excellent in terms of the outcome for that individual child, we are robbing Peter to pay Paul in terms of not having sufficient carers to go around. It takes a long time to reinvest in a new carer to bring them up to the same level of expertise as the short-term carer who has now become a permanent carer.* (Fostering, dual)

Placing children with independent fostering providers (IFPs) for long-term and permanent placement

It was very clear from the survey that IFPs are active providers of permanent placements, although they vary in terms of the proportion of their placements that are permanent. Additionally, local authorities vary in terms of the extent to which they use IFP placements for children with long-term or permanent care plans.

There were three main reasons that practitioners gave for children being placed in the independent sector on a long-term/permanent basis. First, there were cases where the child had been placed with an IFP carer on a short-term basis, subsequently needed a long-term placement and was settled: 'Fifty per cent of our ST placements remain as LT placements' (IFP questionnaire). Children would, in many cases, remain with that carer, even if there were additional costs.

If a child has been seen to be thriving there, then good child care practice dictates that that child should be able to remain, regardless of the financial implications to the authority. (Fostering, dual)

However, a number of local authority practitioners viewed the independent sector with some concern and felt that, for example, sometimes they put pressure on their carers to take children on a long-term/permanent basis, even if the child was not well settled, because of the guaranteed placement for the organisation.

The same IFAs who come back to us in the middle of care proceedings and have said to the Guardian, you know, 'The foster carer wants to keep the child'. And it just sometimes concerns me really about what those motivations are . . .' (Fostering, dual)

However, concerns were expressed by IFPs that in some cases local authorities prefer not to consider a beneficial placement continuing because of the cost.

The second important reason identified by practitioners for purposefully turning to the independent sector to provide long-term/permanent placements was that IFPs sometimes had carers with the expertise to care for children who had specific needs,

We have done in the past, particularly for, say, a young person where there is a disability and we don't have a carer in house that can meet that child's needs long-term. (Fostering, single)

This also included needing to place a child out of county, 'Probably in particular circumstances whereby we don't want the child to be in the local area.' (Fostering, single).

Another reason identified for placing children with IFPs in long-term or permanent placements was because at times local authorities simply did not have enough placements in-house: 'If we hadn't got anything in house, then we would approach the private sector' (Fostering, single).

Some local authorities commented that they were reducing the need to turn to the independent sector for long-term/permanent placements and the number of IFP placements they had was decreasing.

Our policy is that in the main we do not use independent agencies. We do use them for very short-term emergency placements, but in the main we don't use them for . . . we would not go out to an independent agency to look for a permanent family. If a permanent family is needed, we need to find those in-house. (Fostering, dual)

Some authorities felt that this ability to limit the use of IFP placements was because they had been more successful in appropriately funding and recruiting new carers of their own, and had had IFP carers move over to them because they were able to offer similar levels of financial support.

Because our fee paying scheme pays quite well, in fact, sometimes it is even more [than an IFP]. We can obviously cut the fee element that goes to the agency, and if they come over to us and they then join our fee paying scheme and we are giving them the fee and all the allowances. More often than not they are better off. (Fostering, single)

The commissioning (local and regional) and contractual arrangements between local authorities and IFPs are constantly evolving and the provision of permanent placements will be an important part of this process. (See further discussion on financing placements – Chapter 7).

7   Supervising, supporting, training and funding long-term and permanent foster carers

The models of supervision and support provided by social workers to long-term and permanent foster carers are another possible way in which local authorities and IFPs might distinguish between services for different kinds of carers and different fostering tasks. Degrees of specialisation, availability of training and frequency of visits do not in themselves tell us about the quality of social work or foster care available in different systems, but they are a necessary part of understanding the range of services linked to different definitions and expectations of long-term and permanent foster care. Funding, too, reflects attitudes and policies in relation to permanence and is an important part of the picture at an organisational, family and child level.

Specialist social work teams and social workers: organisation and training

There were different approaches to organising fostering services with different degrees of specialisation. Some fostering services, particularly in smaller local authorities and IFPs, had teams that covered all tasks from recruitment and preparation to supervising and supporting the full range of carers, while other agencies had separate teams for recruitment/ preparation and for supervision/support (see Chapter 6 for further dis- cussion of specialisation). Within those agencies which had this degree of specialisation, there were some services which had gone further and separated out supervision and support for long–term/permanent carers and for task-centred/short-term foster carers. It also seemed that a third kind of specialisation was emerging, where permanent foster care was included alongside adoption services.

Questionnaires asked if agencies had social workers or teams who specialised in supervising and supporting long-term or permanent foster carers. In response, 40 per cent (30) of local authorities and 27 per cent (18) of IFPs stated that they did have separate teams or workers supporting long-term/permanent carers. (These figures seem high. We suspect that some agencies meant that they had separate teams for supervision generally rather than for long-term/permanent placements.) There were no significant differences between IFPs and local authorities or between single and dual systems. Three dual system authorities stated that they had a team for permanent foster care, but not for long-term foster care.

There were 43 per cent (32) of authorities and 48 per cent (30) of IFPs which provided their social workers with post-qualifying training specific to long-term or permanent foster care. There was a significant difference between whether an agency had specialist teams or workers and whether they provided post-qualifying training, with 62 per cent (18) of authorities with more specialised services provided post-qualifying training compared to 33 per cent (14) of authorities which did not have specialist teams or workers;[19] 82 per cent (14) of IFPs with separate teams provided post-qualifying training compared to 33 per cent (15) of IFPs which did not have separate teams.[20] This is perhaps unsurprising considering that a long-term/permanent specialist team might be expected to have additional expertise in long-term/permanent foster care support, and therefore be likely to have undergone more training. However, it may also suggest a need for social workers who support a mixture of placement types, who are the majority, to have some specialist training on permanence.

The questionnaire and interview comments suggested that specialist teams and workers fell into three types. The first was teams that were entirely committed to supporting long-term/permanent foster care. Carers in one of the focus groups were very keen on this system and felt that as long-term carers they were getting elite treatment, such was the quality and focus of the support.

---

[19] $\chi 2 = 6.10$, $df = 1$, $p<0.05$
[20] $\chi 2 = 11.91$, $df = 1$, $p<0.01$

A second type of team or group of workers simply tended to focus more on long-term/permanent cases:

[There is a] small group of link social workers whose workloads are weighted towards the assessment, support, supervision and review of long-term carers. (Questionnaire, fostering, single)

Having specialist workers rather than teams was fairly typical of the IFPs, who tended to be smaller agencies where staff might flexibly take up roles to which they were best suited.

Some staff are very good at the crisis management of the early bridge needs/court proceedings and others are very good with taking a deep/long/slower route. (Questionnaire, IFP)

In some local authorities there appeared to be "virtual teams" with just one or two workers from each generic team, who specialised in long-term/permanent foster care, but between them shared expertise in long-term/permanent cases

The other type of team was where long-term/permanent foster carers were supported by the adoption and permanence team. One authority with the dual system, for example, had amalgamated permanent foster care with the adoption and permanence team, leaving long-term cases with task-centred or "temporary" placements. Here again we see the age differentiation and the different lesser expectations of teenage placements.

The permanence support team includes permanent and family and friends foster carers, adoption support and special guardianship. Long-term (13+) are supported as temporary carers. (Questionnaire, fostering, dual)

Most authorities which had separate, specialist teams said that they thought it worked well. Long-term/permanent carers' support needs were said to be met more effectively because the team was very familiar with the needs of long-term/permanent placements.

It works well as it ensures focus remains on supporting specific place-ments. It identifies and pre-empts potential challenges. (Question-naire, fostering, dual)

However, practitioners from other agencies, local authorities and IFPS, stated that, because the majority of foster carers are task-centred, it was not viable to have a team devoted to long-term/permanent carers.

We had that kind of differentiation and it resulted in very unbalanced case loads really so we moved away from it. (Fostering, single)

Other practitioners stated that, if they separated out support for different types of placement, the social workers would not be as familiar with the carers and children, as carers often had mixed placements and most long-term/permanent placements had evolved from short-term.

I think that there is a better flow of task-centred through into long-term because my workers get to know their families and know whether they can do the long-term task. (Fostering, single)

Support and supervision practice

We were interested in both the frequency and the focus of foster carer supervision to see if specialist permanence practice was developing – or was thought to be needed.

Frequency of visits

Table 7.1 shows the frequency with which social workers were said to visit task-centred and long-term/permanent foster carers. There was no means of knowing whether this was the policy on frequency of visits or the actual frequency, but on these figures, there were no differences between single and dual systems in either local authorities or IFPs. This suggests that even those dual authorities which promote a distinction between long-term and permanent foster care consider that they need similar levels of supervision and support.

Agencies were asked to compare long-term/permanent placements with task-centred ones and again there were no statistical differences between the frequency with which social workers were said to visit task-centred and long-term/permanent placements. The majority, around 60 per cent, of both local authorities and IFPs visited their carers every month or six weeks. Some IFPs were more likely to visit carers more frequently, with around a third of IFPs visiting their carers fortnightly compared to almost no local authorities, a statistically significant difference.[21] Around a third of authorities visited their carers every three months compared to less than 10 per cent of IFPs.[22] Three local authorities and no IFPs visited their foster carers less than every three months.

Table 7.1
The frequency of social worker visits to foster carers

Supervision frequency	Agency type	Task-centred (LA n = 74, IFP n = 64)	Long-term permanent (LA n = 73, IFP n = 67)
At least fortnightly	LA	1%	1%
	IFP	36%	30%
At least monthly or six-weekly	LA	68%	58%
	IFP	59%	61%
At least every three months	LA	27%	37%
	IFP	5%	9%
Less than every three months	LA	4%	4%
	IFP	0	0

The interview data also suggested that long-term/permanent placements tended to receive the same frequency of visits from supervising social workers as short-term placements; however, some local authority practitioners did acknowledge that if the placement was running smoothly there could be scope to reduce the number of visits, regardless of the placement status:

> *It happens in temporary foster care sometimes too, when you are looking at a period of stability and the support needs are minimal then, you know, how much supervision/ support do you need to offer? So I don't think it is about priorities, I think it is more about where that placement is up to. (Fostering, dual)*

---

[21] $\chi 2 = 22.23$, $df = 1$, $p<0.01$
[22] $\chi 2 = 15.24$, $df = 1$, $p<0.01$

Some IFPs also took this attitude in the questionnaire and had flexibility when it came to supervising long-term/permanent placements e.g. 'Frequency may reduce by agreement between all parties' (Questionnaire, IFP). However, other IFPs had clear-cut polices: 'The fortnightly supervision is not negotiable' (Questionnaire IFP). IFP workers were more likely to visit long-term/permanent foster carers more frequently than local authority workers and commented that frequent supervision was necessary because the needs of the children in their care were more complex: 'Monthly visits are not negotiable as children placed with us have multi-dimensional and complex needs' (Questionnaire IFP). Whatever the frequency, fortnightly or monthly, IFPs agreed that the status of the placement did not change the need for supervision as the children still have the same needs, a view that many local authority workers would also agree with.

> It is [IFP] policy for foster carers to have supervision every two weeks ... we do not expect any type of fostering to present less challenges or issues regardless of type of placement. (Questionnaire IFP).

IFPs with more frequent visits believed that this reduced disruption of placements.

> There is evidence that fortnightly frequency can provide stability and does reduce crises and emergencies especially outside normal office hours. (Questionnaire IFP)

In this context, the emphasis on frequent visits achieving stability for the child seemed to outweigh any risk that frequent visits might discourage a sense of family membership in long-term/permanent placements which were running smoothly – an argument sometimes used for reducing the frequency.

In the focus groups, foster carers stated that the frequency of visits tended to be reduced when they began to look after a child on a long-term/permanent basis. When this was not with their agreement or by negotiation, they felt unsupported and undervalued as a result. As elsewhere, terminology is critical for carers' self–esteem.

We are classed as "low maintenance" situations which they don't need to bother with. 'We are sorry we haven't seen you for three or four months, but you are low maintenance', that is what they said. We are low priority. (Foster carer)

However, some of the long-term/permanent foster carers commented that they liked reduced visits, because it allowed them to "get on with things". What seemed to matter was that they felt consulted, and commented that they had a flexible system with their social worker and the support was there if they needed it.

To me as long as there is somebody at the end of the phone I don't wish to have anybody visit me. That is because the placement is fairly settled, I don't want them calling. (Foster carer)

However, other foster carers stated that they appreciated regular visits and actually needed that level of support: 'I see my link worker and I find that I can offload onto her' (foster carer). Whether visits are frequent and routine or more flexible and responsive to need, foster carers want to know that their social worker is available, if needed, and supervising social workers need to keep up regular telephone contact to demonstrate their continuous interest and availability.

Focus of supervision

As with the issue of specialisation in organisation and training, it seemed possible that agencies might vary in the extent to which they adapted the focus of supervision in the context of the permanence plan. The survey findings suggested that for 39 per cent (28) of authorities and 40 per cent (25) of IFPs, the focus of supervision was seen to differ between task-centred and long-term/permanent foster carers. There was a significant difference between single and dual systems, with 65 per cent (15) of authorities in the dual system stating that the focus of the supervision differed compared to 27 per cent (13) of authorities with the long-term single system.[23] Unfortunately, it is unknown whether there was a

---

[23] $\chi2 = 9.47$, $df = 1$, $p<0.01$

difference between long-term and permanent within the dual system as this question was not asked. This was no significant difference between the IFP single system (35%, 7) and dual system (43%, 18). Unsurprisingly, more local authorities with separate long-term/permanent teams stated that the focus of supervision differed (56%, 15) compared with those which did not have separate long-term/permanent teams (29%, 12).[24]

Many practitioners commented that the focus of the supervision changed depending on the placement's specific needs rather than the type of placement: 'All carers and children and relationships are unique and most seek appropriate help as required' (Questionnaire, IFP). However, some practitioners stated that there were features of supervision common to long-term/permanent placement which differed from short-term placements, because the task was different and the support needs were different. One practitioner commented that 'long-term is about effecting developmental change over a period' (Questionnaire, fostering, single). Another practitioner commented that, in supervision, 'Identity may figure more prominently with permanent carers' (Questionnaire, fostering, single). One IFP practitioner commented, 'There is more focus on therapeutic/life story work needs'.

This practitioner suggested that supervision would have some overlapping areas but differ in key respects, for example, dealing with different contact issues.

> *Although essential tasks are similar, the focus for long-term will be on establishing security within the placement for the young person, maintaining established ties with birth parents. In short-term, it will involve dealing more with uncertainty. There may be very frequent contact and disruptions caused by that.* (Questionnaire, fostering, single)

Additional to identity and contact issues, some practitioners felt that supervision in long-term/permanent placements should be forward looking and focus on future needs for the child and the foster family.

---

[24] $\chi 2 = 5.02$, $df = 1$, $p<0.05$

You need to focus more on the future needs of the child and the life course of the foster family. (Questionnaire, IFP)

Post-approval foster carer training

Given that many short-term carers might become long-term carers later in their fostering career, it seemed important to consider the status of post-approval training specific to long-term/permanent foster care.

Table 7.2
Post-approval training offered to foster carers

LA	Agency type	Single *(LA n = 51, IFP n = 20)*	Long-term dual *(LA n = 25, IFP n = 45)*	Permanent dual *LA n = 25, IFP n = 41)*
Post-approval training specific to LT/P offered to foster carers	LA	45%	28%	32%
	IFP	45%	49%	46%

There were no significant differences between single and dual systems, although there was a trend for long-term carers in single system authorities to receive more training than long-term and permanent carers in the dual system. There were no significant differences between whether local authorities had specialist teams or workers and whether they offered specialised training to carers. However, there was a significant difference among IFPs with 72 per cent (13) of IFPs with a separate long-term/permanent team or workers providing specialist post-approval training compared to 58 per cent (18) of IFPs which did not have separate long-term/permanent teams or workers.[25]

---

[25] $\chi 2 = 5.67$, $df = 1$, $p<0.05$

Training accessed by long-term and permanent carers

It seemed possible, given the emphasis on settled placements and long-term/permanent foster carers providing a "normal family life", that there might be differences in terms of numbers accessing post-approval training.

Table 7.3

Post-approval training accessed: how often LT/P carers access post-approval training compared to ST carers

LA	Agency type	Single *(LA n = 49, IFP n = 20)*	Long-term dual *(LA n = 26, IFP n = 44)*	Permanent dual *LA n = 25, IFP n = 43)*
More	LA	0	0	4%
	IFP	10%	5%	2%
Same	LA	57%	46%	44%
	IFP	85%	84%	86%
Less	LA	25%	31%	28%
	IFP	5%	9%	10%
Don't know	LA	18%	23%	24%
	IFP	0	2%	2%

Around a quarter of authorities stated that long-term/permanent carers accessed training less than other carers compared to fewer than 10 per cent of IFPs.[26] The great majority of IFPs reported that long-term/permanent carers accessed training at the same level as other types of carers, compared to around half of local authorities, a significant difference.[27] It is not clear if this is a resource issue, in terms of the provision of training, or has more to do with training expectations associated with different terms and conditions of employment for IFP carers. But it was also apparent that local authorities with many more carers than most independent agencies had more "don't know" responses, suggesting

---

[26] $\chi2 = 12.43$, $df = 1$, $p<0.01$
[27] $\chi2 = 26.26$, $df = 1$, $p<0.01$

perhaps greater difficulty in monitoring foster carers' attendance at training relative to their approval status and the plans of their foster children.

Content and purpose of post-approval training

Authorities which ran separate training courses specific to long-term/permanent fostering commented that there was a need for a specific course because the aspects of the fostering task were different to other types of fostering. Many of those which did not run training courses felt it would be a good idea for this reason.

I think we need to do more in terms of specific training for carers wanting to do long-term work, because it is a different task. (Fostering, single)

Practitioners from authorities which had separate post-approval training said that this training looked at managing contact over the years, children's development, identity and carer commitment from a long-term/permanent perspective. One practitioner commented that the permanence training had been received very favourably.

The long-term/permanent carers are better informed and we have tailored some training to their specific needs. So we have looked at permanence options, resilience, we have looked at contact. We have used research in terms of what works and what doesn't work and put that into the training . . . the feedback has been excellent and I think it has also been good that we've actually been able to listen to their experiences too. (Fostering, single)

It seems that long-term/permanent carers benefited from sharing learning and also sharing their particular experiences with each other and with agency staff.

Almost all the practitioners interviewed commented that adolescence could be problematic in long-term/permanent placements, even in placements which had previously been running smoothly. This linked very much to the kind of qualities that carers were said to need. Some practitioners commented that specific training on long-term/permanent foster care could increase carers' commitment and prepare them for the challenges of adolescence:

Once you say to a child you're going to be here long term, the foster carer's got to be absolutely sure. Because you can take a child at seven it's easy, but long-term training is needed for what to expect when they're teenagers and going through their adolescence, especially when their early life impacts on that time. So I think looking forward and the importance of committing to the children, the importance of making sure before carers do commit to them. Placement breakdowns are further rejection, aren't they? Yes, I could think of all sorts of things to go in a training course for long-term carers. (IRO, dual)

Two practitioners from dual system authorities said that they had brought in specific training for permanent foster care, but not for long-term foster care, because permanent foster care had a much more structured matching and approval route. They commented that the permanence task was different to long-term foster care, because the commitment was to provide a stable home into adulthood with the expectation of full family membership and close relationships with the foster carers. Training was therefore necessary in order to make sure that the carers would be fully committed to the placement throughout its duration:

The permanency training talks about their motivation and their expectations, what is different about permanence as opposed to mainstream fostering. It is about balancing their understanding of the life experience of children who need permanence. It looks much more in-depth at areas like loss and separation, disruption and the impact of this on children and how they can manage to maintain a sustained relationship for the child placed permanently. It is about being very clear about the message that this is about taking children into adulthood. (Fostering, dual)

In setting up this training only for permanent foster carers, long-term foster carers in this authority appear to be seen as making a different, lesser commitment and so to need less training in some key areas. But given what is likely to be the backgrounds of those children – often teenagers as we have seen – who receive long-term foster care plans in dual system authorities, it seems that carers would need very similar understandings of separation and loss, the impact of disruption and the importance of helping young people into adulthood. The commitment might be for a shorter period of time and the involvement with the birth family might be greater – but the parenting of the young people must be rather similar in its aims.

Supervision, support and training for BME carers

The preference for matching children on the basis of culture and ethnicity in any placement, but particularly in permanent placements, led to a survey question about whether specialist services were provided for black and minority ethnic foster carers. Table 7.4 shows the extent to which specialised supervision, support services and training for BME carers were offered by local authorities and IFPs. Fewer than one in five local authorities and IFPs offered supervision, support services or training specifically for BME carers or in a non-English language. Most of these authorities and IFPs were based in London, Midlands and Wales. There were no significant differences between local authorities and IFPs and between single and dual systems.

Table 7.4

Specialised supervision and support services for BME and non-English language speakers

	Agency type	Supervision	Services	Training
BME specific	LA	7%	17%	16%
	IFP	13%	16%	9%
Non-English	LA	17%	16%	19%
languages available	IFP	10%	16%	13%

LA supervision and services n = 77, BME specific training n = 73, Non-English training n = 64

IFP supervision and services n = 67, BME specific training n = 65, Non-English training n = 63

This area of practice obviously needs to be tailored to local need. Providing separate and specialist services for BME carers may be necessary and helpful in some areas more than in others. A range of different cultural attitudes to permanence, including attitudes to birth family contact, for example, would still need to be taken into account in general training programmes and some local authorities and IFPs did mention that this was their practice.

Financial support for foster carers: fees and allowances

In considering the role of foster carers as providers of long-term/ permanent placements, who are expected to offer children a place in their family through to adulthood, the question of financial support needed to be explored in terms of both agency and carer expectations. This tricky issue overlaps inevitably with earlier discussions in relation to role definitions, the place of the independent sector – and to the wider question of whether foster carers who provide a family for life are to be treated as "professionals". The issue also connects with the debate (see Chapter 8) about the financial support likely to be offered to carers who apply for special guardianship orders or to adopt the children in their care.

Allowances paid to carers

An allowance refers to the set amount that the foster carer gets paid to cover the actual cost of looking after a child. There are nationally recommended rates set by the Fostering Network. Around one in five authorities (21%, 16) and rather fewer IFPs (14%, 9) stated that the rate for allowances changed depending on the type of placement. There were no significant differences between systems or agency type.

Fees paid to carers

The amount and structure of fees paid to carers has become an important issue in fostering services generally, but has particular significance in relation to long-term/permanent care, as both carers and agencies may commit themselves to particular terms and conditions at the beginning of what is expected to be a long placement.

The vast majority of authorities (91%, 71) and IFPs (92%, 61) paid their carers fees in addition to allowances, with no differences between single and dual systems. Of those who paid fees, only six per cent (4) of

Figure 7.1
Basis for different levels of fee – Local authorities and IFPs

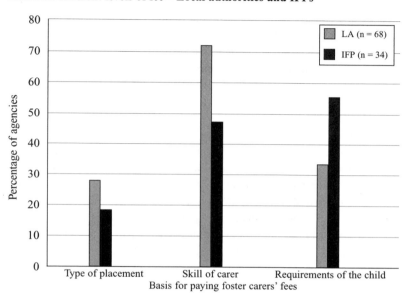

authorities paid all their foster carers the same level of fee compared to 48 per cent (30) of IFPs, which was a significant difference.[28] Figure 7.1 indicates the basis for paying certain levels of fee to carers, including long-term/permanent foster carers.

There were no differences between single and dual systems in local authorities and IFPs which paid varying levels of fees. Around only a quarter of authorities (27%, 18) and a fifth of IFPs (18%, 6) stated that fees were paid dependent on the *type* of placement (short-term/long-term/permanent). The interview and focus group data confirmed that this was not as frequent as payment based on *skills* or requirements of *the child*. But where authorities did decrease the amount of fees for a long-term/permanent placement, it could make a big difference.

People have gone from short-term to long-term and the money drops by about £50 a week. (Foster carer)

---

[28] $\chi2 = 31.31$, $df = 1$, $p<0.01$

Of course there are less obvious ways in which the type of placement might impact on conditions and income in the longer term. Where carers have made a commitment to a particular child in a certain local authority or IFP, they are effectively tied to those terms and conditions thereby making it difficult if not impossible to transfer to a different agency. Thus a carer's personal and professional commitment to caring long-term for a child or sibling group in middle childhood on low fees might mean that, although fellow carers can move on to higher rates with another agency, you – and your children – get left behind in terms of income and, potentially, quality of life.

The findings from this study on the basis for payment of different levels of fees showed some perhaps surprising differences (Figure 7.1). Almost three-quarters of local authorities which paid different fees based this on the *skills* of the carer (72%, 49). However, only just over a third of IFPs (47%, 16) made fee levels dependent on the skill of the carer, this difference was significant.[29] In contrast, just over half of IFPs (56%, 19) who had varied fee levels stated that fees depended on the *requirements of the child* compared to a third of local authorities (34%, 23) (although this difference was not significant).

What is interesting here, and may highlight some differences of attitude and approach in local authorities and IFPs, is that local authorities have moved in the last 10 years or more away from basing fee payments on the level of difficulties in the child, preferring to use a structure that reflects skills and the increasing professionalisation of foster care; for example, expecting carers at higher fee levels to demonstrate their skills and learning through undertaking NVQ. Local authorities had identified the fact that, with structures which relied on the level of children's difficulties, there was a risk that carers would be penalised financially for improving a child's behaviour and development. There was also a recognition that it was difficult to distinguish degrees of child difficulty, since as thresholds to care were raised, almost all looked after children had significant difficulties. It also meant that carers who had previously cared for a difficult child but then had a less difficult child placed with

---

[29] $\chi2 = 6.13$, $df = 1$, $p<0.05$

them might have a sudden drop in income. Although not all local authorities have adopted the same framework of "payment for skills", the principle is now the most common basis for fees payment.

A greater number of IFPs, including those who paid different fees on the basis of the child's difficulties, appeared to have taken a different approach – although further investigation of this point would be necessary to track the underlying reasons. It seemed possible that IFPs were making the assumption that all their foster carers were equally skilled. Thus any differentiation in fee, in those that took a differentiated route, needed to reflect a difference in the task, not the carer. So that in placements where children required a notable difference in time and energy, perhaps needing the carers to accompany them on frequent trips to hospital or to be in frequent attendance at school, the carers could legitimately be entitled to an additional fee. One IFP commented that it was important that this was a transparent process, recognised as fair by their carers.

Of course this differential by carer skills or by child difficulty is not as clear-cut as this discussion makes it seem. In practice, where there is a payment for skills system, more skilled carers are likely to be given more challenging children to care for. Similarly, children who lack obvious behavioural problems may be placed with less experienced or less skilled carers.

Local authorities and IFPs mentioned that other factors which might sometimes influence the fees included the child's age, the length of time the carer had been working for the agency, the number of siblings in a sibling group, and the availability of beds. Some IFPs added that there were regional variations in their fee structure, which may have emerged from the commissioning process with different local authorities.

Financial arrangements between local authorities and IFPs

Even though most local authorities and IFPs did not pay their long-term/permanent foster carers allowances and fees that were different from those paid to short-term/task centred carers, almost half of IFPs (48%, 31) stated that they had different financial terms and conditions with local authorities where long-term and permanent placements were provided.

Comments in the questionnaire indicated that these different financial terms and conditions were usually a slightly reduced fee paid by the local authority to the IFP, which was said not to affect allowances and fees to carers.

It is never a reduction of the young person's allowances or carers' fee; it is always the management's fee. (Questionnaire, IFP)

Sometimes this policy was actually a set amount, e.g. '10 per cent reduction of fee for permanent carers' (Questionnaire, IFP), whereas other IFPs looked at the cases on an individual basis; e.g. 'I will make agreements for discount on permanency arrangements in certain cases' (Questionnaire IFP). Sometimes the discount was given on condition that the placement had been matched and taken to panel, presumably to ensure that the placement was planned and would remain with their agency and that funding would continue throughout. Yet other IFPs reduced the payment if the placement had simply been running smoothly and it was unlikely the child would be moved, e.g. 'If the placement is stable after the first year they [local authority] receive a 7.5 per cent reduction of fee' (Questionnaire, IFP).

In this area of policy and practice there seemed to be very different – and strongly held – views. Some IFPs take for granted that placement costs are negotiated in long-term/permanent placements, while others were obviously angered by the question, asking why they should be reducing the fee to local authorities when the service the child needed would be the same. This is a complex market for local authorities and IFPs, as well as complex in terms of placement definitions and expectations. The nature of commissioning and tendering, and emerging regional commissioning arrangements, will all have an as yet unknown impact on financial arrangements for placements that are planned to be permanent.

Other support for long-term and permanent carers

In addition to supervision, finances and training, local authorities offered other types of support specific to long-term and permanent foster care. One of these resources was different kinds of support groups for long-term/permanent carers, which both practitioners and foster carers said were successful because carers who were in the same position and really understood the role of a long-term or permanent carer could support each other.

They are a group of carers with the same commitment in terms of they have all made an undertaking to offer permanence to a child and are all struggling to various degrees to maintain that emotional commitment and that physical commitment and, you know, the sharing of their home and everything that goes with it really. Sometimes against quite challenging odds, other times it is a much more settled placement. There is a whole range within that group but they certainly have been able to support one another, I think, because the level of empathy and understanding of the issues is huge. (Fostering, dual)

Some of the foster carers spoke of social gatherings, which allowed their children to meet other children and for the carers to meet other carers. They also spoke of formal awards and other occasions which helped them feel valued:

We have a lot of social gatherings for the children in our care as well as our own children. And also we have what we call a Gala Evening, for just the carers and their partners and then you get a certificate for ten, fifteen, twenty years and a massive bouquet of flowers as a thank you to us for the work we are doing. (Foster carer)

Another type of support offered to long-term/permanent carers was respite care (more correctly referred to as "short-breaks"), with some differences in the way that local authorities and IFPs approached this area of practice. Some local authorities said that they were aiming to consider it for every long-term / permanent placement as part of the plan from the beginning of the placement. They felt it might avoid disruption later on.

It is our intention now when we plan a long-term placement to look at where there is a need for respite to be built in right from the beginning, because we have found that, as soon as things become difficult and we try to put in respite, it is almost a self-fulfilling prophecy for that child – 'No I am not going to stay here, I must be going to move again' and you know that placement breaks down. (Fostering, single)

IFPs also quite commonly provide respite care in any placement. Some practitioners felt strongly that respite care was unsuitable for long-term/permanent placements, because it was the aim for the child to feel part of a normal family, but recognised that it was difficult to have a rigid rule about this.

> If carers are committing to permanently looking after a child and that child is going to become, to all intents and purposes, part of their family, you don't ship your own children off to strangers, do you, for four weeks of the year while you go off on holiday or whatever? But I know some placements do need that provision in order to survive really. I am not saying we won't offer it, what I am saying is when we are thinking with our carers about what offering long-term for this child means, we will be starting from the premise that this child is going to become a member of your family – how would you handle that need if it was your own child? (Fostering, dual)

The question of respite care is one of the most difficult issues, for children but also for carers, social workers and planners. Not only is the terminology problematic, with its implication that the child is so difficult that carers/parents need "respite" or even a "short break", but there are very different practices. At best, practice includes pairing foster families, so that the child is known and comfortable in both families and spending time with the non-resident foster family would seem quite natural and not so unlike ordinary families. As well as continuity of respite carer, foster carers and children should be encouraged to keep in touch while they are apart, by phone or by text.

At worst, there are children who go to different respite families each time and never get to go on holiday with the rest of the foster family. The key issue seems to be whether there are other children in the family and how the child experiences and is able to manage different treatment. Although most children would find it difficult to be "sent away", there are children and teenagers who go once a month or for part of school holidays to a family where they can do activities and have experiences that they can not have in the foster family. These more productive models of "respite care" need to be developed more widely.

Most practitioners felt that there should be a flexible approach to respite care. Although it is not desirable in all cases, it obviously needs to be made available for some children and families, but available in the least disruptive and most constructive form possible. Similarly, although making respite care the norm may be right for some foster families, it would be equally unhelpful to force families who are settling a child into a secure routine to have the child removed for a break that neither the child nor the carers need or welcome simply because this is policy. Flexible practice based on good assessments of children and carers is essential.

8 Other permanence options for foster carers: focus on special guardianship

Although this study has a focus on care planning for permanence for children who remain in foster care and looked after by the local authority, the fact that the law provides for further options that foster carers may take to change their status in relation to the child is an important issue to be considered. If carers make certain choices or certain options are promoted by local authorities, this will in itself affect how permanence in foster care develops.

Adoption for foster carers is a familiar option and will be discussed briefly below. But of major interest to agencies and to the research team was the new possibility of special guardianship in England and Wales, provided for in the Adoption and Children Act 2002, implemented in December 2005. In offering a legal status short of adoption, special guardianship might be seen as potentially appealing to foster carers who had already committed themselves to caring for a child as part of their family through to adulthood. On the other hand, if local authorities were to focus too much on special guardianship as a route out of care and take up was low, it might simply detract from developing practice for those who remain in foster care. Lowe and Murch *et al* (2002, p. 148) certainly raised this concern, suggesting that the problems caused by the absence of positive policies for the use of long-term foster care 'seem likely to us to be further exacerbated by the proposed introduction of the special guardianship provisions of the Adoption and Children Bill'.

This combination of potential interest and concern meant that specific questions needed to be asked in the questionnaire, in interviews and in the focus groups to see if it was possible to gauge some early developments in relation to the interface between long-term/permanent foster care and special guardianship.

Special guardianship

The introduction of a special guardianship order has provided a legal route by which parental responsibility for a child up until the age of 18 can be obtained without ending the parental responsibility of the birth parents. The order gives special guardians the right, as local authorities have under a care order, to limit the exercise by birth parents (and others) of their parental responsibility. Birth parents cannot apply for the order to be discharged without leave of the court, thus offering some security to the special guardians and the children in their care. But parents can return to court *without leave* to apply for other orders, such as for contact (see Jordan and Lindley, 2006, for more detail).

The most obvious implications for a foster child if the foster carers were to make a successful application to become special guardians are that the child would no longer be "in care", reviewed every six months and so on; special guardians will have greater powers to act in a parenting role for the child; and the child's place in the family is confirmed by a court as expected to last at least up until 18. Many local authorities in this study were hoping that special guardianship as a permanence option would be quite widely taken up by both family and friends and unrelated foster carers. Some local authorities were even anticipating a drop in numbers of children in long-term care as a direct result of this new provision.

It is important to bear in mind that special guardianship may be part of a local authority plan for a child to achieve permanence outside of the care system, but it is very different legally and procedurally from a care plan for adoption. A placement for adoption is made under a Placement Order with approved adopters, changing the child's status to that of "placed for adoption" and giving adopters parental responsibility even before the adoption order is made. But a child cannot be "placed for special guardianship" in the same way; the child simply remains in foster care until the foster carers initiate the application for a special guardianship order. Even then, the court may well decide that the child should remain looked after by the local authority and in foster care. If a local authority decision were to be made that special guardianship was the right plan for a child, but the present foster carers were not prepared to consider it, a move to another foster placement (apart from the risk to the child if the separation were to disrupt a secure attachment), would not necessarily lead to a successful application.

Foster carer focus groups commented that although some carers may be keen to make this commitment to a child in their care, they were concerned about the loss of earnings in households where fostering income is essential, the loss of money and benefits for the child (for example, for activities, for therapy, when a child is leaving care or at university) and the loss of support and advocacy which might be needed for children who have multiple special needs that require financial resources. Concerns were also expressed about managing contact, and although the Adoption and Children Act specifically mentions the importance of a local authority offering support for contact, legally the special guardians are in the same position as a parent with a residence order after divorce – if a contact order is in place but not going well, they would need to go back to court to change it, with the associated distress and cost. These issues will be discussed in more detail.

Take up of special guardianship

Special guardianship was frequently mentioned in the social work interview data as an important option, although it was approached with a combination of interest and caution by many practitioners. At this time (January–June 2007), SGOs had only been used by most authorities for kinship carers and the number of non-related foster carers making an application was reported to be low.

> *In terms of SGOs we have actually made 11 on children who were looked after and another six were granted on children in need. For children in need, it was all family members and of the 11 for looked after children, ten orders were to family members, one was to a previous foster carer as in not known to that child before they went into their care. So in our situation the vast majority of SGOs are being made to family members.* (Fostering, single)

Some practitioners mentioned that their agency had already provided foster carers with information about SGOs and the feedback had been fairly positive.

We have made sure that foster carers have print outs and handouts about special guardianship so they understand how it would apply to them if they wanted to make an application to care for a child that they had been looking after. We have made sure that they have got all of the information they need. (Fostering, single)

Potential advantages of special guardianship for foster carers and children

One of the main reasons some practitioners thought that long-term/permanent carers might take up the order was that it meant there would be less involvement from social workers and would give the carers more parental responsibility – meaning that the placement would function more like an ordinary family.

On the whole, children don't like social workers. Even social workers they like, they don't like the fact that someone visits them at least four times a year, they don't like the fact that there are meetings about them twice a year, they don't like the fact that they can't do, or they feel they can't do lots of things, they need permissions and consents, the fact that someone is a "foster carer" as opposed to Emma or David or something else, even if they call them by their first names, they have still got that title. Long-term care, I think social services can take their eye off the ball. But if actually they don't need much from us, then shouldn't we find a better solution? People like me hope that special guardianship might offer a way forward so that we can have fewer children in care and rather more children having more normal family arrangements. (LAC, single)

Several practitioners commented that if a placement was stable and had been working for a period of time, they would encourage the long-term/permanent foster carer to take out a special guardianship order for these reasons.

For a number where they have been in place for some time and everything is good and they are settled at school and you think, well, us having to do our six-weekly visits and having two annual reviews and having to probe, you know, the kids, they don't want that. They don't want that and we certainly don't want that for them. So if we matched a child permanently to foster carers, we are always asking the question in the review process, would you consider a special guardianship order? (Fostering, single)

The legal security of special guardianship is clearly in itself going to appeal to some foster carers who are concerned that birth parents, or indeed social workers, could challenge their right to be the child's long-term carers and who want to give a positive message to the child.

Potential disadvantages of special guardianship

One of the reasons practitioners gave for thinking that special guardianship may not be appropriate for some long-term/permanent placements and not attractive to carers was that some carers needed guaranteed ongoing support for the child's special needs or contact needs, especially where relationships with the birth parents were not good.

There are a couple of foster families where they said, 'No, I have got a disabled child and I am not sure that I would be able to fight as effectively if I were just a parent. I want the local authority's backing on things and if the child is in public care then there is more clout.' But in the majority of cases it's purely finance. The other thing that might put them off is sharing PR with the birth parent. If the birth parent is particularly difficult, that would put them and the child maybe in a vulnerable position. (Fostering, dual)

Foster carers expressed their concerns about support, especially in the future.

I think with special guardianship the danger is going to be right from the beginning. It is going to be agreed at the beginning and they are not going to take into account anything else at all. Anything that might come up in the future, you know, mental health issues. They are saying there is such a high incidence of mental health problems in LAC children. A lot of mental health issues don't show themselves until adolescence, teenage, puberty and if you are taking on a two-year-old and agreeing you are going to manage these – and then by the time they turn 12 they are needing extra this and extra that and trips to here and therapy there. (Foster carer)

But the main reason cited by nearly all practitioners and most of the foster carers for a likely low take up of special guardianship orders by local authority and IFP carers was that most carers would lose at least some if not all of their financial support. As one carer put it, 'I would be happy to do it if the financial package remains the same as it is now.' The authorities had differing financial arrangements for SGOs, but for the majority they meant a reduction of fees and allowances at some point.

I think carers are all committed to the children, but it is purely finance. That is the feedback I have had from the carers, it is purely finance. You know they are committed to that child anyway, but it will make it a lot harder if they didn't have the finance at the level they are already receiving it. (Fostering, single)

Almost a quarter of local authorities stated that their approach to financing special guardianship was under review (24%, 16). Where it had been agreed, in most authorities financial support would be means tested and expected to end after two years, as suggested by Government, unless there were exceptional circumstances. At this stage it seems likely that only a small minority of local authorities will provide support packages equivalent to the full allowances and fees which foster carers currently receive. Indeed, less than one in five local authorities (18%, 12) stated that they could maintain carers' current fees and allowances for the duration of the child's placement if they were granted special guardianship. The rest had various schemes such as making decisions on an individual basis, keeping the fees and allowances for two years then reducing them via means testing, paying an allowance similar to the residence order or adoption allowance or a combination of these. Some arrangements were rather unappealing, as in this foster carer's story of being expected to rely on benefits.

It was suggested to us that we apply for [child] and how they suggested it to us was that they would calculate what our earnings are now, as you would when you get means tested, as to how much money did we need and then pay us a percentage and the rest would be topped up with Family Credit. That is what they suggested to us. (Foster carer)

Some practitioners reported that even though the allowances for carers may have to reduce, children would still receive their leaving care entitlements.

Basically one of the issues that has prevented some carers who maybe wanted to go for SGOs on kids they have been caring for a long time is the loss of the young person's leaving care entitlement. So what we said is, they will be entitled, in terms of supporting their further education i.e. they go to University, the financial aid we would give etc. in terms of equipment and a grant, that will be maintained even if they do become subject to an SGO and therefore cease to be looked after. (LAC, single)

The risk of a drop in financial support was an important issue for IFP carers, as well as the potential loss of support through the relationship with the fostering agency. Some local authority practitioners felt that children who should be on a permanent order, such as an SGO, continued to be looked after because they were placed with an IFP carer.

Because, let's face it, it is a no brainer for an IFP carer where we have already agreed the child can remain there permanently. There are one or two carers that would still do it, because of how the child has become part of their family. But there is a lot that wouldn't because they rely on that income. (LAC, single)

This situation will, however, also apply to many local authority foster carers, for whom fostering is their career and their main or only source of income.

More generous support packages

There were a few local authority practitioners who suggested that, if long-term/permanent carers took up special guardianship, their authority could maintain the same financial support if that was what the carer wanted.

We guarantee that a carer would not lose out financially moving from long-term foster care to special guardianship in terms of our allowances. (LAC, single)

One authority had a project where they had actively approached their permanent foster carers whose placements were suitable for special guardianship with the offer of full support (financial and social work support) if and when they needed it. This project had been undertaken twice and most of those that had been approached took up the offer.

We saw that we had a number of foster carers who are very committed to the children that they looked after, some of them were, you know, eight, nine-year-olds, ten-year-olds, for whom the plan was that they were not going to return home and for whom adoption was less likely to occur, as well as teenagers who have been in placement for some time. On discussion with some of those carers that expressed an interest, they said that yes they would want to secure some permanency for the child they were looking after, but they could not afford not to have an income from fostering. So we had a special project and identified those children and those carers who felt that this was a possibility for them and we supported them financially through that and have continued to support them on the fostering rates. (Fostering, dual)

Practitioners from two authorities who could offer full support for special guardianship stated that the independent providers were reluctant to support their approach to carers.

The other difficulty we have experienced is with some of the independent fostering agencies and their reluctance obviously to support special guardianship for children. That isn't a blanket comment; it is more about particular agencies than a general view. But we have had a spot of trouble with that really and I have to say our view would be that they are possibly seeing their relationship with their foster carers as more important than the outcome for the child which is very concerning. (LAC, single)

A practitioner from another authority which could offer greater financial and other support had also had success with special guardianship and had had over twenty long-term/permanent carers take it up because permanence was actively on the agenda and promoted by a permanence officer.

I think that [financial support] is a critical aspect of it, I also think that the fact that we do have a Permanency Officer whose job it is to make sure that these matters are progressed has been very helpful. His role is to sort of join with the social worker and the supervising social worker and ensure that matters are progressed to some form of permanency outcome if that is appropriate. (LAC, Single)

A practitioner from one authority stated that maintaining a high level of support had actually been criticised by the court.

Certainly quite a lot of our in-house carers and some of our IFP long-term carers are looking towards SGOs. We are in a bit of a dilemma at the moment, because we are attracting a bit of criticism from the courts, saying that we are offering people too much support when they go for SGOs. They are questioning whether we are legally entitled to offer that level of support financial and practical, which seems a bit strange really. (LAC, single)

However, even with the maximum financial and other support being offered, practitioners believed that the majority of long-term/permanent placements would not be suitable for special guardianship orders because of the ongoing needs of the placement. But practitioners also highlighted the fact that some long-term/permanent carers did not want to take it up because they viewed themselves as a foster carer rather than the child's parent or guardian.

I think it would be a small number and the ones I am thinking of are experienced carers who have been caring for a long time. They may be moving on from being carers in the not too distant future but, you know, are committed to the children they have got placed with them. Whereas other carers see their role as a job, you know. They want these children to come and live with them for a period of time and they move on and others join them, I don't think those ones would look at special guardianship in the same way. (LAC, Single)

Adoption

Foster carers adopting children in their care is a more established route to permanence and fewer comments were made regarding this option. Just under 10 per cent of authorities (9%, 6) stated that they would be able to offer the same fees and allowances if carers adopted. The vast majority said that carers would be means tested for the adoption allowances, with some allowing a two-year buffer (80%, 53). The remaining authorities had various schemes which involved a reduction of fees over a time period. (A detailed study of pathways to permanence, including long-term foster care, adoption by strangers, adoption by carers and special guardianship is being undertaken at York University, led by Professor Nina Biehal and funded by the Department for Children, Schools and Families.)

9 Summary of findings and key messages for policy and practice

Key findings

- **Using data from 93 local authorities and 67 independent fostering providers (IFPs) in England and Wales, this study has provided evidence of the existence and characteristics of diverse local authority models for planning for permanence in foster care**. Although there are two identifiable local authority models i.e. single systems for long-term *or* permanent foster care (61%) and dual systems for long-term *and* permanent foster care (39%), data from the questionnaire survey, interviews with staff and foster carer focus groups suggest that there is a great deal of diversity within as well as between systems.

- **Differences exist in the first instance at the level of definition**, with authorities distinguishing between placements intended to last until leaving care from those intended to last into adulthood. This range could apply to both "long-term" and "permanent" foster care placements.

- **The age of the child was a critical factor in definitions and systems**. Younger children (up to age 6 or 7) were expected to be placed for adoption if at all possible, although sibling relationships and other factors affected this decision. Middle childhood children (approximately 6–11) were more likely to be placed for permanence in the dual system authorities, but in both dual and single systems there tended to be greater expectations of foster family membership through to adulthood for this age group. Adolescents (12–18) were, both explicitly in procedures and implicitly in terms of practitioner expectations, generally thought to have less need of foster family membership and a permanence plan.

- **Both single and dual care planning systems have the potential to be inclusive of the full range of age and need, but this range needs to be explicit in policy and practice.** Dual systems may be at risk of treating long-term foster care as a lesser and inferior option. Single systems need to take care to ensure a focus on permanence for the full range of children. Both systems need to address the needs of adolescents as well as younger children.

- **The legal status of the child was a factor in decision making, but almost all local authorities would make long-term and permanence plans for children who were accommodated (s20) as well as for children on care orders (s31).** Where there were co-operative relationships with birth parents, in the interests of the accommodated child, this could work well. Concerns were raised, however, about practice for accommodated children where birth parents were entirely absent or obstructive and local authorities felt unable to act fully as parents. This also affected some unaccompanied asylum-seeking children, who were likely to be accommodated.

- **The expected balance between the role of foster carers and the role of birth parents for children of different ages and in different placements was an important part of definition and planning.** This issue was often expressed in terms of two different concepts – "loyalty" and "attachment". These concepts were often blurred and the term "strong attachment" to birth parents was used to suggest that some children as young as six or seven would not be able to become full members of foster families and that many teenagers in particular would not wish to. This seemed to be based on the (erroneous) idea that children cannot form multiple attachments. Thus, underlying different systems and practices were explicit and implicit assumptions about children's developmental needs.

- **These different care planning systems and definitions were linked to different planning procedures.** Most marked were differences between local authorities in the **choice of panels** to make best interests and matching decisions. This ranged from looked after children reviews or planning meetings through to fostering panels and adoption and permanence panels. Fostering panels were the most commonly used decision-making forum. Only a small minority of local authorities used the adoption and permanence panel for foster care, and this was more common for permanent foster care placements in dual systems. Most practitioners welcomed decision making beyond the LAC review to ensure **a higher level of external scrutiny**, a degree of **specialist expertise** – and to give **clear messages** to children, to carers and to birth parents about the expectations of the placement.

- **Practice varied also in the nature of the documentation used for best interests and matching decisions**. This was sometimes but not always linked to choice of panel. The **child's permanence report (CPR)**, the standard documentation in adoption, was used by around 50 per cent of local authorities. Some practitioners found it less suitable for foster care, but most wanted fostered children to have the same degree of detailed assessment as adopted children. Although more likely to be used for permanent foster care and for cases going to adoption and permanence panels, the CPR was also used for long-term foster care cases going to fostering and other panels. There was variation in the use of medical and school reports across and within different systems.

- **Family and friends carers were often included in the same systems as unrelated carers, once formally approved as carers**. In some local authorities, they were less likely to be classed as permanent, while in others they were allocated to teams within the adoption and permanence service. Most authorities were working to manage family and friends placements outside of the care system where possible – whether through informal arrangements or through special guardianship.

- **Social work practice with children was generally described as not very different from that with short-term fostered children**, because of the legal requirements, although **visiting** might be less frequent when placements were well settled. Concern was expressed in some local authorities and by IFPs at the frequent changes of social worker experienced by some children. Practitioners also expressed concern that **life story work** was not routinely available to foster children (63% of local authorities) as it was in adoption.

- **Negotiating parental decision making about day-to-day matters in children's lives was challenging, with a great deal of variation in what decisions foster carers might be able to take.** This variation was not linked to different definitions and systems in long-term/permanent placement planning, but often depended on an individual team or social worker. There was thought by most social workers and carers to be a need for both more powers delegated to foster carers and greater clarity about decision making.

- **Looked after children reviews were seen as playing an important part in working towards achieving a permanence plan.** However, there was general concern about the fact that **independent reviewing officers** and the review system generally needed to take more account of the permanence plan once placements were established. Reviews, for example, were still asking every six months why the child was not going home, causing upset to children and carers – and probably birth parents. In addition, when new social workers or IROs had not properly familiarised themselves with the history and the plan, decisions could be made at reviews (e.g. increasing contact) that were in breach of the letter and the spirit of the care plan.

- **Leaving care services undoubtedly play a critical role in supporting many young people in the transition to adulthood.** Social workers and foster carers raised certain concerns, however, about a lack of differentiation in leaving care practice. Some young people who were settled in planned long-term or permanent placements were being offered accommodation and support to be "independent" without sufficient consideration given to the child's place in the foster family or the role of the foster carers as parents.

- **Data on recruitment, approval, supervision and support of long-term and permanent foster carers reflected some variations in approach that cut across different care planning systems.** First, there were some inevitable differences in practice and procedure between carers who were changing from short-term to a long-term/permanent role for a child already in their care or for a child new to the family. However, most local authorities undertook a process of reassessment and "matching" in existing placements. Secondly, there were very mixed views on whether carers new to fostering should be approved to take long-term or permanent placements without prior experience of short-term fostering. This issue polarised opinion among social workers and carers.

- **There was agreement that the foster care task in long-term and permanent placements needed particularly high levels of skill, commitment and resilience**. There was some concern expressed in most local authorities and IFPs about the availability of enough suitable long-term and permanent foster placements to ensure **placement choice** and **a good match**.

- **There was mixed reporting of the benefits of having more specialist recruitment and supervision/support teams**. Specialisation may relate to recruitment or to recruitment of long term/permanent carers. It was recognised that if there was specialisation it was important for there to be good communication between teams.

- **Special guardianship was seen as an important new option for foster carers (especially family and friends carers), but carers had concerns about losing financial and other support for themselves and the children**. Some local authorities had hopes that this option may reduce overall numbers in long-term care, but others were very aware that the terms they were able to offer foster carers would not be acceptable and would potentially disadvantage carers and children. Only a few authorities were offering terms equivalent to current fostering fees and these were hopeful that this would work well for carers and children.

Key messages for policy and practice

- Whatever the care planning system for permanence in foster care, it must address the developmental and permanence needs of all children, including adolescents. The current approach to adolescents needs to be challenged.

- Systems, procedures and practice need to be underpinned by explicit and accurate understanding of children's development and relationships and of the current research on foster care and permanence.

- All meetings and panels involved in decision making need to be provided with appropriately detailed assessment documentation for best interests, approval and matching decisions – and to have the appropriate knowledge and expertise to use it as a basis for their decisions.

- LAC reviews need to be very carefully managed in the light of the care plan, with children's case records clearly marked with the status of the placement. Children's progress does need to be reviewed but with sensitivity to the child and the placement.

- Social work practice with children during care planning and through the years of a long-term or permanent placement requires skills and continuity. Life story work should be routine. Leaving care practice needs to be sensitive to the needs of individual children and carers in different foster families.

- Social work practice with carers needs to acknowledge the special role that carers have in being entrusted with parenting children through to adulthood. Placement agreements and LAC reviews need to be tailored to the parenting role that they play. Scrutiny of the placement has to be balanced with the permanence plan.

- Practice with birth parents needs to be focused on enabling them to play as constructive a role as possible in the child's life, maximising the benefits and minimising any risks to the child's development and placement.

N.B. These messages for policy and practice are explored in more detail in *Achieving Permanence in Foster Care: A good practice guide* by Gillian Schofield and Mary Beek (BAAF, 2008)

The need for further research

- This study was the first national study of care planning systems for permanence in foster care. It was able to provide detailed accounts of policy and practice in a wide range of agencies and also to offer some useful perspectives from social workers and foster carers. However, the study was primarily descriptive. It was not able to comment on the strengths and limitations of practice in different systems.
- What is needed is research offering a more detailed analysis of practice and outcomes for children, in particular, an investigation of assessment and decision making, linking and matching, support and supervision in different local authorities and care planning systems.
- Since completing this study, a grant from the Nuffield Foundation has been awarded to a team at the University of East Anglia (Gillian Schofield, Clive Sellick, Mary Beek and Emma Ward) to undertake this further study (2008–10).

References

Beek, M. and Schofield, G. (2002) 'Foster carers' perspectives on permanence: a focus group study', *Adoption & Fostering* 26:2, pp. 14–27.

Beek, M. and Schofield, G. (2003) 'Tuning in to children: Providing a secure base for children with severe learning difficulties in long-term foster care', *Adoption & Fostering* 28:2, pp. 8–19.

Beek, M. and Schofield, G. (2004a) *Providing a Secure Base in Long-Term Foster Care*, London: BAAF.

Beek, M. and Schofield, G. (2004b) 'Promoting security and managing risk: contact in long-term foster care', in Neil, E. and Howe, D. (eds) *Contact in Adoption and Permanent Foster Care: Research, theory and practice*, London: BAAF.

Cairns, B. (2004) *Fostering Attachments*, London: BAAF.

Department for Education and Skills (2004) *Every Child Matters*, London: The Stationery Office.

Department for Education and Skills (2007a) *Care Matters: Time for Change*, London: The Stationery Office.

Department for Education and Skills (2007b) *Looked After Children Statistics 2005–6*, London: The Stationery Office.

Farmer, E., Moyers, S. and Lipscombe, J. (2004) *Fostering Adolescents*, London: Jessica Kingsley Publishers.

Howe, D. (2005) *Child Abuse and Neglect: Attachment, development and Intervention*, Basingstoke: Palgrave Macmillan.

Jordan, L. and Lindley, B. (eds) (2006) *Special guardianship: What does it offer children who cannot live with their parents*, London: Family Rights Group.

Kearns, K. A. and Richardson, R. A. (2005) *Attachment in Middle Childhood*, New York: Guilford Press.

Kohli, R. K. S. and Mitchell, F. (2007) (eds) *Working with Unaccompanied Asylum Seeking Children: Issues for policy and practice*, Basingstoke: Palgrave Macmillan.

Lowe, N. and Murch, M., Bader, K., Borkowski, M., Copner, R., Lisles, C. and Shearman, J. (2002) *The Plan for the Child: Adoption or long-term fostering*, London: BAAF.

Performance and Innovation Unit (2000) *Prime Minister's Review of Adoption*, London: The Stationery Office.

Ryan, T. and Walker, R. (2007) *Life Story Work* (3rd edition), London: BAAF.

Schofield, G. (2000) 'Parental responsibility and parenting: the needs of accommodated children in long-term foster care', *Child and Family Law Quarterly* 12:4, pp. 345–362.

Schofield, G. (2003) *Part of the Family: Pathways through foster care*, London: BAAF.

Schofield, G., Beek, M., Sargent, K. and Thoburn, J. (2000) *Growing up in Foster Care*, London: BAAF.

Schofield, G. and Beek, M. (2006) *Attachment Handbook for Foster Care and Adoption*, London: BAAF.

Schofield, G., Thoburn, J., Howell, D. and Dickens, J. (2007) 'The search for stability and permanence: modelling the pathways of long-stay looked after children', *British Journal of Social Work*, 35, pp. 1–24.

Schofield, G. and Beek, M. (2008) *Achieving Permanence in Foster Care: A good practice guide*, London: BAAF.

Selwyn, J., Sturgess, W., Quinton, D. and Baxter, C. (2006) *Cost and Outcomes of Non-infant Adoptions*, London: BAAF.

Sinclair I (2005) *Fostering Now: Messages from Research*, London: Jessica Kingsley Publishers.

Sinclair, I., Baker, C. and Wilson, K. (2005) *Foster Children: Where they go and how they get on*, London: Jessica Kingsley Publishers.

Sinclair, I., Baker, C., Lee, J. and Gibbs, I. (2007) *The Pursuit of Permanence: A Study of the English care system*, London: Jessica Kingsley Publishers.

Stein, M. and Carey, K. (1986) *Leaving Care*, Oxford: Blackwell.

Stein, M. (2008) 'Leaving Care', in Schofield, G. and Simmonds, J. (eds) *The Child Placement Handbook: Research, policy and practice*, London: BAAF.

Thoburn, J. (1991) 'Survey findings and conclusions', in Fratter, J., Rowe, J., Sapsford, D. and Thoburn, J. *Permanent Family Placement: A decade of experience*, London: BAAF.

Thoburn, J. (2007) *Globalisation and Child Welfare: Some lessons from a cross-national study of children in out-of-home care*, University of East Anglia, Norwich.

Thoburn, J. (2008) 'International contexts and comparisons', in Schofield, G. and Simmonds, J. (eds) *The Child Placement Handbook: Research, policy and practice*, London: BAAF.

Thoburn, J., Norford, L. and Parvez Rashid, S. (2000) *Permanent Family Placement for Children of Minority Ethnic Origin*, London: Jessica Kingsley Publishers.

Wade, J., Mitchell, F. and Baylis, G. (2006) *Unaccompanied Asylum Seeking Children: The response of social work services*, London: BAAF.

Wilson, K., Sinclair, I. and Petrie, S. (2003) 'A kind of loving: A model of effective foster care', *British Journal of Social Work*, 33, pp. 991–1003.